THE CRIMES OF
STALIN
THE MURDEROUS CAREER OF THE RED TSAR

NIGEL CAWTHORNE

ARCTURUS

PICTURE CREDITS

RIA Novosti: **6, 8, 9, 18, 21, 23, 27, 28, 34, 35, 36, 37, 38, 43, 44, 46, 49, 50, 52, 55, 57, 58, 59, 60, 61, 62, 63, 65, 73, 74, 81, 82, 83, 84, 88, 89, 90, 92, 95, 96, 97, 98, 102 (2), 103, 104, 105, 106, 109, 110, 115, 116, 117, 118, 120, 125, 127, 128, 130, 131, 135, 137, 139, 140, 145, 147, 149, 150, 152, 157, 160, 163, 165, 166, 168 (2), 170, 171, 173, 174, 175, 176, 178, 180, 182, 183, 184 (2), 188, 198, 199, 201**

Shutterstock: **12, 20, 29, 31, 42, 47, 56, 81, 86, 101, 128, 144, 151, 153, 154, 165, 169, 172, 202**

Corbis: **13, 30, 194, 196, 200**

Getty Images: **78**

Topfoto: **134 (2)**

David Woodroffe: Map pp.**10–11**

Mirco De Cet archive: **40, 54**

State Historical Museum, Moscow: **16**

Bundesarchiv: **146**

We have endeavoured to contact the copyright-holders of all images used in this book. Any oversights in this regard will be rectified in future editions

ARCTURUS

This edition published in 2011 by Arcturus Publishing Limited
26/27 Bickels Yard, 151–153 Bermondsey Street,
London SE1 3HA

Copyright © 2011 Arcturus Publishing Limited

ISBN: 978-1-84837-580-2
AD001260EN

Printed in China

CONTENTS

INTRODUCTION

When Stalin died, his legacy was twofold: he was father of the Soviet Union, a superpower with a huge sphere of influence, but all his achievements had been built on untold human misery

I WAS BORN TWO YEARS BEFORE STALIN DIED, SO I WAS NOT ABLE TO WITNESS HIS ACTIONS AT FIRST HAND. Nevertheless, I have seen some of the effects of Stalinism. In 1989 – before the Berlin Wall came down – I was stuck in Moscow with a suitcase full of United States documents. They related to the CIA, the National Security Agency (NSA), the US Department of State and the US Department of Defense. At the time, I had been finishing a book about the American prisoners who had disappeared after the Vietnam War. While I was there I received a telegram from the government in Hanoi inviting me to discuss the matter. My advance was already exhausted, so I decided to travel cattle-class on Aeroflot, taking the documents with me to demonstrate my knowledge of the subject.

However, I missed my connection in Moscow, which meant that I spent three days in a gloomy transit block with various stateless people who seemed to have got lost in the system. There was a concierge on each floor keeping a gimlet eye on everyone and we were only given thin soup to eat. No one was allowed outside. Even though the grim apartment blocks of the city could only be glimpsed from the coach that took me back and forth to the airport, it was easy to see how people could simply disappear.

The next time I visited Russia was in 1993, after the Berlin Wall had been brought down. I was writing a book about the British prisoners of war who went missing in the Second World War. When the Red Army 'liberated' them from the German prisoner of war camps in the east they did not return to the United Kingdom because they had been sent to Stalin's Gulag – the system of slave labour camps that ringed Russia.

On that trip I visited Vorkuta, a huge mining settlement in the Arctic Circle, where I knew prisoners had been taken. There is no road to Vorkuta, just the railway that runs up from Ukhta. Begun in 1941, it was built by prisoners. The train journey takes 12 hours and it is said that there is one corpse for every sleeper. During the winter the ground was frozen, so the dead could not be buried. Instead, their bodies were stacked at the side of the tracks until the brief summer thaw came, when a thin layer of soil was sprinkled over them. After a time, their white bones would poke through the earth. They were left that way because the local people were told that those who had died were 'enemies of the people'. And just to remind everyone who was responsible, each rail had the name 'Сталин' – Stalin – cast on its side.

The mines and camps of Vorkuta were surrounded by miles of barren tundra cut by rivers, ponds and marshes, which spread as far as the horizon. This vast expanse of scrub and marshland was patrolled by the local inhabitants, who were given food and ammunition in exchange for the heads of runaway prisoners. The dead bodies of runaways were displayed at the watch posts for three days, as a warning to others. For most of the year the area was frozen and impassable. Even in June there were still huge banks of snow, though the sun did not set, day or night. During Vorkuta's years as a penal colony, not a single person successfully escaped.

Around the town were the remnants of the 60 camps that had supplied labour for the mines there. Officially, each camp held between 1,800 and 2,400 prisoners, but they often accommodated four or five times that number. At the height of the Stalinist era there were 7,000 free men in Vorkuta – people who had completed their sentence but had remained in exile there, together with guards and railway workers.

Many of the camps nestled in the crook of a fast-running river that had ice floating in it, even in midsummer. The far bank was steep and exposed, which presented would-be escapees with another formidable obstacle. Some of the prison barracks were still inhabited. The huts that had been designed for 70 men had been restyled into charming terraced cottages by covering them with wooden slats, which were then plastered and painted pink. These must have been desirable residences when they were freshly converted, provided that the occupants were not troubled by sleeping there. Others had been left to decay, the earth insulation spilling from their walls.

Iron cages, where prisoners might have been left to die of exposure, were still intact. And under the stone-built guard houses one could still see the tiny, unheated punishment cells. These were so small that the detainees could neither stand up nor lie down. The captives were left to squat in the freezing cold for days on end after committing such heinous crimes as trying to draw a picture on a torn piece of canvas with a lump of coal.

The watchtowers still stood at the corners of the work compounds, which were surrounded by four concentric barbed wire fences. There was no reason for such elaborate security precautions. Even if a prisoner got through the wire, there was nowhere to run to.

Beyond the compounds were graveyards stretching as far as the eye could see. The anonymous grave markers were still in place, but their cross-pieces carried no names, for the dead were just identified by a letter and two digits, such as A46 or R87. When the gravediggers reached the end of the alphabet, they would start again at A00. This helped minimize the scale of the deaths in the minds of the people who worked there. But why did they bother? Why did they not just throw all of the dead into a mass grave? The answer is that individual graves legitimized the whole process. The Soviets persuaded themselves that they were not butchers like the Nazis, because the men who were worked to death in Stalin's labour camps had been tried and sentenced individually, as enemies of the people.

An exhibition dedicated to the camps was being held at the local town hall, where the cheery hostess announced that 20 million people had died in Vorkuta, this town that was just 50 years old. The local representative of the Memorial – the organization for Gulag survivors – thought this was something of an overestimate. The Memorial estimated that as many as 60 million people had died in the Gulag, and they maintained that Vorkuta was by no means the biggest of the penal colonies. Nevertheless, the death toll was such that Stalin must count among the greatest killers of all time, the equal of Adolf Hitler and Mao Zedong. Not that this would have worried him, for one of the statements attributed to the dictator is: 'A single death is a tragedy, a million deaths is a statistic.'

This is not the avuncular figure who was dubbed 'Uncle Joe' by Second World War propagandists when he was an ally of Britain and America. At that time he saw himself more as a

From the 1930s, Stalin's forced labour camps began to spread round the coalmining town of Vorkuta. In 1953, an uprising there was brutally quelled

'The Red Army along with our allies' forces will break the backbone of the Fascist beast' – Stalinist poster, 1943

knight errant, so his favourite films were Sergei Eisenstein's *Ivan the Terrible*, which portrayed the first tsar, and *Alexander Nevsky*, the story of a 16th-century Russian prince who beats off the German attackers.

True, Stalin did see off the German invaders in the Great Patriotic War of 1941–5, as the Russians called it – that is, the Eastern Front in what we in the West refer to as the Second World War. But he was often more of a hindrance than a help to his generals. In the 1930s, Stalin purged the Red Army of most of its competent officers, which led to the sacrifice of millions of ill-trained, ill-equipped men. And in 1939 he even embraced Hitler. If he had maintained his alliance with Britain and France – and left his army intact – Hitler might have thought twice about attacking Poland and the Second World War might not have happened. As it was, Stalin always turned against those who supported him, so the friends who had helped him to power were rewarded with a bullet in the head. On a far greater scale, millions of innocent people were deliberately slaughtered by the minions who had been issued with execution quotas and others were starved to death or deported from lush agricultural soil to barren regions in the east or the north.

Stalin's great creation, the Soviet Union, collapsed in 1991. More properly known as the Union of Soviet Socialist Republics (USSR), it was essentially the old tsarist empire, which the Communists took over in 1917. At its height, it embraced Armenia, Azerbaijan, Belorussia (now Belarus), Estonia, Georgia, Kazakhstan, Kirgiziya (now Kyrgyzstan), Latvia, Lithuania, Moldavia (now Moldova), Russia, Tajikistan, Turkmenistan, Ukraine and Uzbekistan. It was the world's largest country, for it extended to two and a half times the size of the United States and covered one sixth of the world's land mass. And over it all – from inside the walls of the Kremlin like some medieval monarch – reigned the Red Tsar, Stalin himself.

Nigel Cawthorne
Bloomsbury, London

Stalin's Empire

(all borders shown are contemporary)

BARENTS SEA

NORWAY

DENMARK
Kiel
Hamburg
GERMANY
Berlin

SWEDEN

LAPLAND

Murmansk

Kola
Peninsula

KAF

Tampere
FINLAND
BALTIC SEA
Helsinki

White Sea

CZECH
REP
Gdansk
POLAND
Warsaw
Krakow
SLOVAKIA

LITHUANIA
Vilnius

ESTONIA
Tallinn

Archangel

White Sea
Canal

LATVIA

St. Petersburg
(Petrograd)
(Leningrad)

Vologda

Solvychegodsk

Komi
Republic

Lvov
Galicia

Minsk
Brest-Litovsk
BELARUS

Smolensk

Vorkuta

ROMANIA
Bucharest

Kiev
UKRAINE
MOLDOVA
Odessa
Kharkov

Kursk

Moscow

RUSSIA

Perm

Sevastopol
BLACK
SEA
Yalta
Kerch

Volga
German
ASSR

Yekaterinburg
(Sverdelovsk)

Samara

Ankara

Volgograd
(Stalingrad
Tsaritsyn)

Omsk

GEORGIA
Batumi
TURKEY
Chiatura
Gori
Tbilisi
(Tiflis)

Caucasus

CASPIAN
SEA

Aral Sea

KAZAKHSTAN

Altay Kray

SYRIA

AZERBAIJAN
ARMENIA
Baku

Kengir

IRAQ

UZBEKISTAN

Alma Ata

Tehran

TURKMENISTAN

KYRGYZSTAN

IRAN

TAJIKISTAN

0   250   500   750 kilometres

0   250   500 miles

BERING SEA

EAST SIBERIAN SEA

Kolyma

LAPTEV SEA

KAMCHATKA

● Magadan

● Norilsk

Arctic Circle

SEA OF OKHOTSK

S I B E R I A

khansk

Achinsk
● ● Krasnoyarsk

Lake Baikal

● Novaya Uda

Irkutsk ●

CHINA

● Vladivostok

MONGOLIA

NORTH KOREA

SOUTH KOREA

CHINA

◼ = labour camps

CHAPTER ONE

THE TYRANT IS DEAD

Stalin ruled over the Union of Soviet Socialist Republics for nearly 30 years. He had been responsible for the deaths of at least 20 million people, he had deported another 28 million and he had enslaved 18 million individuals in labour camps, yet some of those who gathered around his bedside were still true believers. Others feared for their lives.

Stalin's 70th birthday party: [from left to right] Togliatti, Budenni, Kaganovich, Suslov, Mao Zedong, Bulganin, Stalin, Vassilevski, Khrushchev, Barruri, Georgeiu-Dej, Shvernik, Malenkov, Beria, Voroshilov, Molotov, Mikoyan and Racosi

ONE OF STALIN'S LAST CRIMES BACKFIRED ON HIM AND HASTENED HIS DEATH. For years the Soviet press, at his behest, had been making constant references to the Jews who lived in the Soviet Union. They were being dismissed from their posts, arrested and executed. The Jews were seen as a 'Fifth Column' – that is, a minority group that might prove disloyal to the USSR. Less than eight years after the death of Hitler and the public exposure of the murderous extent of the Holocaust, Stalin planned to round up all of the Jews that remained in the Soviet Union – many of them survivors of the Nazi death camps – and then transport them to Siberia in cattle cars, where two new concentration camps had been built for the purpose. An engineer saw one of these camps in the 1960s. He described 'row after row of barracks' that had never been used.

'Its vastness took my breath away,' he said.

The Doctors' Plot

Seventy-three-year-old Stalin had long mistrusted Jews, so he intended to rid his vast empire of them, thereby succeeding where Hitler had failed. He also mistrusted doctors. In 1927 Stalin consulted the world-renowned psychologist Vladimir

Bekhterev, a rival of Pavlov. He was depressed after a power struggle with Leon Trotsky, a Jew. The good doctor concluded that Stalin was suffering from 'grave paranoia', a mental illness, which was a little unwise because he died immediately afterwards – poisoned on Stalin's orders – and Stalin then had his name removed from the textbooks.

Under the last tsar Jews had not been allowed to own land or pursue certain careers. However, they were permitted to become doctors, so a disproportionate number of them had joined the medical profession. This gave Stalin an opening. His plan was to stage one of his famous show trials.

On 13 January 1953, the daily newspaper *Pravda* (Truth) announced that nine of the Kremlin's top doctors had been arrested for murdering two of Stalin's closest aides some years earlier. In an article called 'Ignoble Spies and Killers under the Mask of Professor Doctors', they were accused of taking part in a vast plot orchestrated by Western imperialists and Zionists. Their supposed aim was the elimination of leading Soviet political and military leaders. They were tortured in order to wring confessions from them.

Meanwhile, there would be a propaganda offensive. A million copies of a pamphlet called 'Why Jews Must Be Resettled from the Industrial Regions of the Country' had been prepared for distribution. A number of leading Jews had also been browbeaten into signing a statement asking for Jews to be deported 'for their own good', which would be published in *Pravda*. The text read:

> *'We appeal to the government of the USSR, and to Comrade Stalin personally, to save the Jewish population from possible violence in the wake of the revelations about the doctor-poisoners and the involvement of renegade Soviet citizens of Jewish origin, who were caught red-handed in an American-Zionist plot to destabilize the Soviet government. We join with the Soviet peoples in applauding the punishment of the murdering doctors, whose crimes called for the highest measure. The Soviet people are naturally outraged by the ever-widening circle of treason and treachery and the fact that, to our sorrow, many Jews have helped our enemies form a fifth column in our midst. Simple, misguided citizens may be driven to striking back indiscriminately at Jews. For this reason, we implore you to protect the Jewish people by dispatching them to the developing territories in the East, where they will be employed in useful national labour and escape the understandably indignant anger prompted by the traitor-doctors. We, as leading figures among loyal Soviet Jewry, totally reject American and Zionist propaganda claiming that there is anti-Semitism in the Soviet Union...'*

'Open letters' were a popular means of persecution in Stalin's Russia. Children had even used them to denounce their parents as 'socially harmful elements', thereby condemning them to the frozen wastelands of Siberia.

One of the signatories of the Jewish letter was quickly sacked from the staff of *Pravda* after a colleague said he could no longer work with anyone who belonged to a race of poisoners and traitors. The Jews began burning their Yiddish books and avoided going out as much as possible, while some committed suicide in anticipation of what was to come. At a small synagogue in Georgia, just a few hundred metres from Stalin's birthplace, the Torah was removed from the Ark so that it could be hidden.

In 1948 and 1949 Stalin had already caused large numbers of Jews to be deported to central Siberia, but this time a worse fate awaited Soviet Jewry. According to Louis Rapoport, author of *Stalin's War Against the Jews*, the doctors were to be convicted and then hanged publicly in Red Square – at a time that would be

POLINA SEMYONOVNA MOLOTOVA (1897–1970)

The daughter of a Jewish tailor in Ukraine, Polina Karpovskaya joined the Russian Social-Democratic Workers' Party of Bolsheviks in 1918. During the Russian Civil War (1918–21), she served as a propaganda commissar in the Red Army. As a Communist she took the revolutionary name Zhemchuzhina, which is Russian for 'pearl'.

In 1921, she married Vyacheslav Molotov, who was by then a member of the Central Committee of the Communist Party of the Soviet Union. She had a successful career in the Soviet administration and was elected a candidate to the Central Committee in 1939.

Stalin began to mistrust Polina when her sister emigrated to what was then the British Mandate of Palestine in the 1920s. Nevertheless the Molotovs and the Stalins shared an apartment and Polina became a close friend of Stalin's second wife Nadezhda.

Polina tried to comfort Nadezhda after she had been publicly rebuked by Stalin during a dinner party in 1932, but Stalin's wife mysteriously died the same night.

During a secret meeting of the Politburo in 1939, Stalin alleged that Polina had 'connections to spies'. She was reprimanded, although no evidence could be found against her, and in 1941 her name was removed from the list of candidates to the Central Committee. After that she actively supported the Jewish Anti-Fascist Committee during the war against Hitler. In November 1948 she befriended Golda Meir, later prime minister of Israel, who was the first Israeli ambassador to Moscow. A month later Polina was arrested, charged with treason, forced to divorce Molotov and sentenced to five years in a labour camp. While she was away Molotov did not dare ask whether she was alive or dead.

After being released from the Gulag so that she could appear as a witness in the doctors' trial, she asked: 'How's Stalin?' On being told that he had just died, she fainted. She was reunited with Molotov and lived with him as an unrepentant Stalinist until she died of natural causes in 1970.

symbolically close to Easter. Then 'incidents' would follow. The secret police would orchestrate attacks on the Jews and the statement begging Stalin for their deportation would be published. A further flood of letters would demand that action be taken.

According to Rapoport,

'A three-stage programme of genocide would be followed. First, almost all Soviet Jews... would be shipped to camps east of the Urals... Second, the authorities would set Jewish leaders at all levels against one another, spying on each other and engaging in provocations. Also the MGB [secret police] would start killing the elites in the camps, just as they had killed the Yiddish writers and intellectuals in August of the previous year. The third and final stage would be to "get rid of the rest".'

The Soviet camps would not need to be turned into efficient Nazi-style death factories, but that was only because the mortality rate in Stalin's camps was so

The dining room where Stalin collapsed. Stalin had the dacha designed by Miron Merzhanov who was to spend 17 years in labour camps. Stalin never trusted anyone — the server of each dish he was brought had to take the first mouthful

appallingly high that the 'Jewish problem' would be solved by attrition.

In preparation for the show trial, Stalin read the daily reports on the interrogation of the tortured doctors sent to him by Semyon Ignatiev, head of the MGB (Ministry of State Security). And he ordered the return of Object 12 – Polina Molotova – the former wife of Stalin's foreign minister Vyacheslav Molotov. Although she had been a loyal Communist since 1918, Stalin had never trusted her because she was Jewish and he frequently suggested that Molotov should divorce her. In 1948 she was convicted of treason on trumped-up charges and sentenced to five years in a labour camp, but that did not prevent her from being an unrepentant Stalinist. Now she was to be groomed to appear as the star witness in the doctors' trial.

Stalin was also moving against his ruthless security chief Lavrenty Beria on the grounds that he had demonstrated a certain lack of vigilance by allowing traitorous doctors to work in the Kremlin. The Red Tsar did not trust Beria because he was a Mingrelian, an ethnic minority in Stalin's native Georgia. Beria's Georgian allies were arrested, along with a former mistress, while his protégés in Moscow were sacked. Beria responded by being disrespectful to Stalin, though he 'expected the death-blow... any minute', according to his son.

On 7 February 1953 Stalin met the Argentine Ambassador Leopold Bravo and asked him about Eva Peron, who had died the previous July. He could not have imagined that within a month he would be dead himself. Then on 17 February he dined with Beria so that he could force him to sign an order attacking the MGB, a move that was designed to rob Beria of allies. He also ordered another assassination attempt on President Tito of Yugoslavia.

Stalin went alone to see the Bolshoi Ballet on 27 February, leaving early. The following morning he read the latest interrogation reports on the Jewish doctors and saw an account of the war in Korea, which was then raging. It seems that he took a steam bath to ease his arthritis, a course of action that his doctors had advised him against. But he had no reason to listen to them now. After watching a film and drinking some Georgian wine, he was driven out to his dacha at Kuntsevo on the outskirts of Moscow. Over dinner his minister of defence, Nikolay Bulganin, briefed him on the stalemate in Korea. Stalin advised the Chinese and the North Koreans to negotiate. Then the conversation turned to the interrogation of the Jewish doctors under chief torturer Semyon Ignatiev, head of the MGB.

'Have the doctors confessed?' asked Stalin. 'Tell Ignatiev if he doesn't get full confessions out of them, we'll shorten him by a head.'

'They'll confess,' said Beria. 'With the help of other patriots like [Dr Lydia] Timashuk' – who had been awarded the Order of Lenin for denouncing her fellow doctors – 'we'll complete the investigation and come to you for permission

As Stalin lay dying, Beria poured forth his bile. Some people still believe he killed the great tyrant

to arrange a public trial.'

'Arrange it,' said Stalin.

It was 4 am before Stalin saw his guests out. He was 'pretty drunk... and in very high spirits'. He lay down on a divan in the dining room and told his chief bodyguard Colonel Ivan Khrustalev that he could have a nap too.

'I won't be calling you,' he said. Khrustalev had never been given the night off before.

Stalin's Illness and Death

At midday on 1 March the guards were awaiting anxiously for Stalin to get up. Although he was a late riser, they grew worried as the day drew on and there were no signs of movement from his apartment. Deputy Commandant Peter Lozgachev was relieved when he saw a light come on at 6 pm. But there was still no summons. Four hours passed. Colonel Nicolay Starostin then told Lozgachev to go in and check that everything was all right. Lozgachev, unwilling to disturb Stalin, protested.

'You're senior, you go in,' he said.

'I'm afraid,' said Starostin.

At 10 pm, a batch of papers arrived from the Central Committee. Lozgachev picked up the documents and set off down the 25-yard-long passageway from the guardhouse to Stalin's rooms. He took care to be especially noisy because Stalin did not like being crept up on. On one occasion a bodyguard had worn slippers instead of boots so he could walk about without waking his sleeping boss, but Stalin had accused him of trying to sneak up silently in order to assassinate him.

In the dining room of the dacha, Lozgachev found Stalin lying on the floor in his pyjama bottoms and undershirt, conscious but helpless. He had wet himself.

'What is wrong, Comrade Stalin?' asked Lozgachev.

Stalin muttered something that Lozgachev could not make out and then lapsed into unconsciousness. Lozgachev immediately called Starostin. With the help of one of the dacha staff, Matrena Butuzova, they lifted Stalin on to the sofa and covered him with a blanket. Stalin's broken watch lay on the floor. It had stopped at

LAVRENTY PAVLOVICH BERIA (1899–1953)

A Mingrelian-Georgian who was born in Azerbaijan, Beria joined the Bolsheviks in March 1917, immediately before the February Revolution. In 1921, he joined the Soviet secret police, the Cheka, who defeated the rival Mensheviks and allowed the Bolsheviks to take over in Georgia and the Transcaucasus. With Stalin's support, Beria then rose to become head of the Georgian Communist Party.

In 1935, Beria published a lengthy treatise called *On the History of the Bolshevik Organizations in Transcaucasia*, in which he emphasized Stalin's role in the region's revolutionary movement. Then in August 1938 Stalin brought him to Moscow, where he became the deputy head of the NKVD (People's Commissariat for Internal Affairs). His chief, the murderous Nikolay Yezhov, was the acclaimed administrator of Stalin's purges, but his position crumbled when Stalin realized the purges were damaging the infrastructure of the Soviet Union and the Party. After taking the blame for the excesses, the unfortunate Yezhov was removed from his position and executed, after which Beria succeeded him. Beria began by purging the secret police and ingratiating himself with Stalin, who praised him by declaring, 'Beria is our Himmler'.

Beria became a candidate member of the Politburo in March 1939 and he was made a Commissar General of State Security in 1941. In his capacity as head of the MVD he recommended the murder of some 22,000 Polish officers, who were killed in the Katyn Forest in 1940. Then following Stalin's orders he carried out a purge of the Red Army and the war industries in 1942. The Gulags under his direction were a major source of raw materials and slave labour, so he was able to take control of armaments production.

After the Germans had been driven from Soviet soil, Beria was put in charge of the deportation of the ethnic minorities, who had been accused of collaborating with the enemy. His organizational abilities were then put to use in a different field. Using agents in the United States and elsewhere, he supervised the building of the Soviet atomic bomb, which entailed slave labourers from the Gulag being sent down the uranium mines. At the same time he was made a marshal of the Soviet Union, though he had never held military rank.

Towards the end of his life, Stalin became suspicious of Beria. He was about to move against him before he died – some think Beria had a hand in his murder. Beria was one of four deputy prime ministers who took over after Stalin's death. Fearing that Beria planned to make himself sole dictator, the other three – Khrushchev, Malenkov and Molotov – moved against him. In June 1953 he was tried as an 'imperialist agent' who had conducted 'criminal anti-Party and anti-state activities'. Convicted, he was stripped to his underwear and manacled to a wall. A towel was stuffed into his mouth to stifle his pleas for mercy and he was shot in the forehead by General Pavel Batitsky, who was promoted to marshal for his pains. His wife Nina was exiled to Ukraine.

Stalin had a film room where he loved to watch newsreels of himself. He also liked to see his image on stamps, leading to a joke of the time about why Soviet stamps didn't stick properly because people kept spitting on the wrong side

6.30 am, so it is assumed that it showed the time at which the stroke had hit him.

Starostin then called Ignatiev, who could easily have called a doctor. Instead he ordered Starostin to contact Beria and the secretary of the Central Committee, Georgy Malenkov. Ignatiev's next move was to call his friend Nikita Khrushchev, who was involved in organizing the genocidal backlash against the so-called 'doctors' plot' and would be in danger from the bloodthirsty Beria if anything happened to Stalin.

Beria was with a mistress. When he was finally contacted, he issued an order. 'Don't tell anybody about Stalin's illness.'

At 3 am on 2 March – five hours after the alarm had been raised – Beria and Malenkov turned up at Kuntsevo. Beria was a little drunk. Malenkov found that his shoes creaked, so he took them off and carried them under his arm as the two of them tiptoed into the dining room, where they found Stalin sound asleep.

Beria berated Lozgachev.

'What do you mean by starting a panic? The boss is sleeping peacefully. Let's go, Malenkov.'

As they tiptoed out, Lozgachev tried to explain that Stalin was gravely ill and needed urgent medical attention. Beria dismissed him as a fool.

'Don't bother us, don't cause a panic and don't disturb Comrade Stalin,' Beria said.

While Stalin remained snoring on the sofa, soaked in his own urine, Beria and Malenkov returned to the Kremlin and began fevered political discussions with Ignatiev, Khrushchev and Bulganin. It was now 12 hours since the stroke, but still no one had called the doctor. No one dared. It has been assumed that Stalin's

Doctor Galina Chesnokova, seen here in 1942, spent three nearly sleepless days by Stalin's bed attempting to save his life, but at 9.50 pm on 5 March 1953 he opened his eyes, raised then dropped his left hand and finally expired...

comrades were jockeying for position and had simply left him to die. However, the 'doctors' plot' and the paranoia it had inspired had gripped everyone in the Kremlin. If they had called a doctor and Stalin had recovered, he could have seen that very act as an attempt to assassinate him. However, simply denying Stalin medical attention might well have killed him.

'I did him in,' Beria later boasted to Molotov and the old Jewish Bolshevik Lazar Kaganovich. 'I saved you all.'

Meanwhile the guards were worried that if Stalin died with no doctor being called they would get the blame. They called Malenkov and he in turn called Beria, who eventually gave in. But first they would have to get the minister of health, Dr Tretyakov, to draw up a list of Russian – that is, non-Jewish – doctors.

Beria, Kaganovich, trade minister Anastas Mikoyan and military commissar Kliment Voroshilov turned up at Stalin's bedside.

'Comrade Stalin, we're here, your loyal friends and comrades,' said Voroshilov.

'How do you feel, dear friend?'

Stalin stirred but could not speak. Later, Beria called his wife Nina and told her that Stalin was dying. She was inconsolable, like most of the Politburo wives – even the ones that Stalin planned to have imprisoned or killed.

At 7 am, a team of doctors led by Professor Lukomsky arrived. None of them knew anything about Stalin's medical history because all of those who had treated him before were now in the hands of the secret police. Lukomsky and his team were terrified by the presence of Stalin and Beria. With trembling hands they attempted to examine the patient and then they gave him some Epsom salt. Afterwards they questioned the guards who were also in fear of their lives.

When they had established that the patient's condition was serious they recommended the application of leeches and a cold compress. He should also be given oxygen and an injection of camphor, they said.

Stalin's daughter Svetlana was called at that point. Beria and Malenkov talked to her, but they did not tell her about the delay in summoning medical help. She noticed that the doctors attending her father were not the ones she had seen before. Shortly afterwards, Svetlana's brother Vasily appeared. He was so afraid of his father

SVETLANA IOSIFOVNA STALINA, AKA SVETLANA ALLILUYEVA (BORN 1926)

The daughter of Stalin's second marriage, Svetlana was just six years old when her mother died. She rarely saw her father. At the age of 16 she fell in love with 40-year-old Jewish filmmaker Aleksei Kapler, who was sent to a labour camp for ten years when Stalin found out. After Stalin's death, the couple were reunited and they had a passionate affair.

When she was 17 years old, Svetlana fell in love with Grigory Morozov, a fellow student at Moscow University, who was Jewish. Her father grudgingly allowed the couple to marry, although he made a point of never meeting the bridegroom. Svetlana gave birth to a son in 1945, but the couple divorced in 1947.

Two years later, Svetlana married Yuri Zhdanov, the son of Stalin's right-hand man, Andrei Zhdanov. Like his father, Yuri was also a close associate of Stalin. The couple divorced in 1952, two years after Svetlana had given birth to a daughter, Yekaterina (Katya).

Following the death of her father, Svetlana became a university lecturer and translated Russian literature into English. On the death of her third husband in 1966, she was given permission to visit his native India. She took the opportunity to defect to the United States where she wrote her memoirs. After moving to England with the daughter of her fourth marriage, she returned to the Soviet Union in 1984, but defected again in 1986. She has spent the remainder of her life in the United States and England.

that he turned up with his airforce maps, but when he realized that the summons was not related to his work he got drunk and began berating the doctors for not saving his father.

With Stalin incapacitated, Beria began to spew forth his hatred of his old comrade, but each time Stalin opened his eyes Beria fell to his knees and kissed his hand, terrified that he would recover. The other members of the Politburo were in tears. Stalin had been in power for nearly 30 years and life without him seemed impossible.

At 10.40 am they met in the Kremlin, leaving Stalin's chair empty. The doctors somewhat nervously gave their detailed report.

'You are responsible for Comrade Stalin's life,' said Beria. 'You must do everything possible and impossible to save Comrade Stalin.'

A roster of those who were to keep vigil – two at a time – was drawn up. Beria and Malenkov were the first. The doctors told them that there was a blood clot on Stalin's brain. He would have remained alive if it had been cleared in time. Beria asked them who would dare to operate on Stalin.

'Who guarantees the life of Comrade Stalin?' he asked.

'No one dared,' Lozgachev said later.

'Death is inevitable,' said the doctors.

Beria could scarcely conceal his delight. At 8 pm that evening there was another meeting in the Kremlin and this time Beria took the chair. By then Stalin

Svetlana, Stalin's daughter, had a house not far from Kuntsevo but had to ask permission to visit her father

was being purged with Epsom salt enemas and fortified spoonfuls of sweet tea. Soon more doctors were drafted in. Stalin's condition was deteriorating, yet the Politburo members needed to keep him alive until they had been able to plan the handover of power. They only had two days in which to divide the spoils, because the next official meeting in the Kremlin was on 5 March.

As it seemed unworkable to have another Georgian in supreme power, it was decided that Beria could not take over. Instead Malenkov would become premier and first secretary of the Communist Party, while Beria was made head of the MGB as well as the MVD (Ministry of Internal Affairs), a position he was to retain. Khrushchev and Bulganin were terrified by the thought of Beria being in charge of the entire state security apparatus, but Molotov was more worried about his wife Polina. He hoped she was still alive in exile but he had never dared to ask. In fact, she had been returned to Moscow and was under interrogation at the MGB headquarters in Lubyanka Square. That evening Beria released her from further questioning, but the doctors would continue to be cross-examined.

Stalin regained consciousness while being fed some soup with a teaspoon. Ignatiev was terrified and Beria again fell to his knees to kiss Stalin's hand. The Russian leader then closed his eyes, not to open them again until his final moments, and at 10.15 am the doctors reported that his condition had worsened.

'The bastards have killed my father,' exclaimed Vasily. Khrushchev immediately began to comfort him.

Beria went home and told his wife that it would be better if Stalin died – otherwise he would be a vegetable. Nina wept.

'You're a funny one,' said Beria. 'His death saved your life.'

As Stalin's condition deteriorated further, the MGB left off torturing the Kremlin doctors and began asking them for their medical opinion. Their prognosis was poor, however, and they had an extremely low opinion of the non-Jewish doctors who had replaced them.

At 11.30 pm, the situation grew critical.

'Take all measures to save Comrade Stalin,' ordered Beria.

A life-support machine was wheeled in, but never used.

On the morning of 5 March, Stalin grew pale and started coughing up blood. By 3.35 pm his breathing had become erratic so Beria sped to the Kremlin to go through his leader's safe and files. He was looking for incriminating documents. Khrushchev and Malenkov joined in the destruction of the papers that implicated them in the Great Terror and the fabrication of the 'doctors' plot'. It is thought that Beria also destroyed any will or political testament that Stalin had left.

That evening a new government was formed under the 'collective leadership' of Malenkov and Beria, who immediately repudiated Stalin.

'That scoundrel! That filth!' Beria shouted. 'Thank God we are free of him.'

Beria denounced Stalin for encouraging the 'cult of personality' and in private he confided that Stalin had not won the war, as the dictator had claimed.

'We won the war,' declared Beria.

He also suggested that without Stalin, 'we would have avoided the war'. Now he was going to expose the 'doctors' plot' which he had opposed, and then empty the labour camps, free East Germany, liberate the various nationalities under Soviet control and open up the economy. Beria also vowed to revenge himself on those who had betrayed him. Many had reason to fear him – not least for his fearsome reputation for brutality.

By condemning Stalin, Beria had left himself open to being denounced as anti-Bolshevik, but one last great show of loyalty was still required. At Comrade Stalin's bedside, Beria announced to the slumbering leader that all the members of the Politburo were there.

'Speak to us,' he begged.

There was, of course, no reaction so Beria invited Stalin's bodyguards and staff to gather round and join the Politburo in saying their goodbyes. The members of the new government then rushed back to the Kremlin, where the new administration was rubber-stamped by the Council of Ministers and the Presidium of the Supreme Soviet. Stalin had officially been replaced as premier, though he was still a member of the Presidium. Everyone was relieved.

At 9 pm Stalin began to sweat and his lips turned blue and at 9.40 he was given oxygen. The doctors suggested an injection of adrenalin to stimulate the heart. They should have asked Vasily and Svetlana, as Stalin's next of kin, but instead they looked to Beria, who ordered it. But nothing now could prevent Stalin's death. He had started

VASILY IOSIFOVICH DZHUGASHVILI AKA VASILY STALIN (1921–62)

The son of Stalin's second marriage, Vasily was sent to aviation school at the age of 17, where he was given special privileges. He rose rapidly through the ranks by denouncing his superiors to his father and by 1945 he commanded an elite air division, holding the rank of general. In spite of his success, Vasily was terrified of his father and he became a drunk and a womunizer. He was even intoxicated when he flew. On one occasion he endangered his passengers and his crew by drinking the aircraft's de-icing spirit, thereby allowing ice to form on the wings. It became necessary to crash-land the aeroplane.

When Stalin heard about Svetlana's affair with Kapler, Vasily was blamed for introducing them and he was demoted, after spending ten days in a guard house. After the death of his father he sensed that imprisonment was inevitable. Sure enough, Beria had him arrested in April 1953. Vasily appealed for clemency when Beria himself was arrested and executed, but to no avail because he was tried behind closed doors and sentenced to eight years' imprisonment. Released in 1960, he died of chronic alcoholism in 1962.

drowning in his own fluids. The death agony was terrible. At the last minute he opened his eyes and looked around wildly.

'It was a terrible look,' said Svetlana, 'either mad or angry and full of the fear of death.'

Then the former tyrant raised his left hand.

'He seemed either to be pointing upwards somewhere or threatening us,' Svetlana related. 'Then, the next moment, his spirit after one last effort tore itself from his body.'

A doctor flung himself on the corpse and began to administer artificial respiration and heart massage.

'Stop it please,' said Khrushchev. 'Can't you see the man is dead? You won't bring him back to life.'

Beria darted forward to kiss the dead body and the others followed suit. Even those under threat of death cried. Only Beria seemed happy as he summoned his car.

'He's off to take power,' Mikoyan said to Khrushchev.

Soon only the family and servants were left. Svetlana was numb. Only Valechka, who had been Stalin's maid for the previous 18 years, showed genuine grief. She lay her head on Stalin's chest and shed the uninhibited tears of a peasant woman.

GEORGY MAKSIMILIANOVICH MALENKOV (1902–88)

Too young to take part in the October Revolution, Malenkov joined the Red Army in 1919. In the following year he joined the Communist Party and during the Russian Civil War he served as a political commissar. He rose rapidly through the ranks and in 1925 he was appointed to Stalin's personal secretariat.

During Russia's Second World War struggle with Germany, Malenkov was one of the five members of the Committee of State Defence. In 1946 Stalin appointed Malenkov as his deputy prime minister after which he became a full member of the Politburo. When Stalin died in 1953, Malenkov assumed the roles of prime minister and head of the Communist Party, though Khrushchev took over as leader of the Communist Party within weeks. Malenkov was a progressive who opposed nuclear armament, fearing it would lead to global destruction, and he called for a higher priority to be given to consumer goods. Khrushchev then condemned him as a revisionist, which forced him to resign as prime minister in 1955.

Malenkov continued as a member of the Politburo but in the summer of 1956 he joined with Bulganin, Molotov and Kaganovich in an attempt to oust Khrushchev. This was unsuccessful and in 1961 Malenkov was expelled from the Communist Party and exiled within the Soviet Union, becoming the manager of a remote hydroelectric plant in Kazakhstan. In his later years he converted to Christianity.

Family man: Stalin with [from left to right] his son Vasily, great friend Andrei Zhdanov, daughter Svetlana and son Yakov. Zhdanov was to become Svetlana's father-in-law when she married his son Yuri in 1949

Was Stalin Murdered?

Russian historian Edvard Radzinski believes that Stalin was murdered. He claims that Stalin was injected with poison by the guard Ivan Khrustalev, under the orders of his boss Lavrenty Beria. The reason was that Stalin was planning another world war.

According to Radzinski,

'All the people who surrounded Stalin understood that Stalin wanted war – the future World War III – and he decided to prepare the country for this war. He said: "We have the opportunity to create a communist Europe but we have to hurry." But Beria, Khrushchev, Malenkov and every normal person understood it was terrible to begin a war against America because the country [Russia] had no economy. It wasn't a poor but a super-poor country which was destroyed by the German invasion, a country which had no resources but only nuclear weapons.'

The dacha's servants share a joke behind Lazar Kaganovich, Georgy Malenkov, Stalin and Andrei Zhdanov. The Soviet leaders would drink deep into the night, before returning to the task of signing death warrants in the morning

Radzinski tied Stalin's plans for the Third World War to the 'doctors' plot'.

> *'It was the reason for his anti-Semitic campaign, it was a provocation. He wanted an answer from America. And Beria knew Stalin had planned on 5 March to begin the deportation of Jewish people from Moscow.'*

Beria, Khrushchev and Malenkov knew that he had to be stopped.

However, there is another theory. The book *Stalin's Last Crime* posits that the blood-thinning agent warfarin was added to Stalin's 'fruit juice' (young Georgian wine). If the right dose had been given over a five- to ten-day period the fatal stroke could have been provoked. Although the doctors' final report neglected to say that Stalin was coughing up blood, it is known that warfarin can produce this symptom.

CHAPTER TWO

KOBA THE PATRICIDE

The autocrat who terrorized the world for 30 years came from humble beginnings. He spent a troubled childhood in Gori, a small town in Georgia, where his father was a cobbler. Although Georgia is now a republic, it was ruled by Tsar Alexander II at the time of Stalin's birth. Gori was a tough town, famous for its street fighters, and the Red Tsar grew up dreaming of the bandits who inhabited the Caucasus. He particularly identified with Koba, the protagonist of the novel *The Patricide*, who kills a village governor.

STALIN WAS BORN JOSEF VISSARIONOVICH DZHUGASHVILI ON **6 DECEMBER 1878.** His official date of birth, however, was 21 December 1879 – or 9 December according to the Julian calendar that was in use before the Communists took over in 1918. It seems that he changed the date along the way in order to avoid conscription.

The house where Stalin was born, which is now covered by a large marble portico in Gori's museum

The Early Years

Stalin's father, Vissarion (Beso) Dzhugashvili, was a drunken, much-travelled cobbler who abused his son Josef ('Soso') and his attractive, young wife Ekaterina (Keke) whenever he had imbibed too much alcohol. Soso was the couple's third child, but their other sons had died in infancy and it looked as if Soso could easily follow them. He was weak, fragile and thin and the second and third toes of his left foot were webbed.

His parents had him christened quickly in case he died. When he survived they

---

THE JULIAN CALENDAR

The Julian calendar was introduced by Julius Caesar in 46BC and it was reformed by Caesar Augustus in 8BC. Like our own calendar, the year was divided into 12 months of either 30 or 31 days, with the exception of February, which consisted of 28 days in a normal year and 29 every fourth year. However, the calendar grew increasingly out of step with the seasons and by the 16th century it was ten days adrift.

In 1582, Pope Gregory XIII corrected the situation by decreeing that the ten days between 5 October and 15 October should be omitted from that year's calendar. In addition, three out of every four centennial years would not be recognized as leap years, thus keeping the new Gregorian calendar in

step with the heavens. Gregory's calendar was quickly adopted in all of the Catholic countries, but for a long time the Protestant nations saw it as the work of the devil. As a result, Germany and most of northern Europe did not accept the Gregorian calendar until 1700 and it was not recognized by Britain and its North American colonies until 1752.

Russia, a hitherto Orthodox country, did not acknowledge the new calendar until 1918, when the Julian calendar was 13 days adrift. Hence, the October Revolution actually took place on 6–7 November according to the Gregorian calendar, whereas the 'old style' Julian calendar showed the date as 24–25 October.

---

took him on a pilgrimage to Geri, just north of Gori, to give thanks.

Keke did not have enough milk to feed the child, so he was suckled by the wives of his godfathers. His mother doted on him and she used his love of flowers to encourage him to walk. Once, when he was attracted by a flower, Keke got her breasts out. Soso ignored the flower and dived for his mother's exposed nipples. Hearing a peeping Tom laughing, Keke quickly buttoned up her top.

The family lived in a two-roomed shack which contained little except for a divan, a table, a kerosene lamp and a samovar. But because his father had a workshop and employed apprentices, Stalin was sometimes forced to admit that he was not the son of a worker but of an exploiter. Stalin's father was sometimes paid in wine and he also did business in the corner of an inn. One of his drinking companions was a Russian political exile called Poka, who was connected to a group that repeatedly attempted to assassinate Alexander II. When Poka was found dead in the snow, Beso began drinking with the local priest, Father Charkviani.

'Father,' begged Keke. 'Don't make my husband a drunk. It'll destroy my family.'

Rumours circulated that Soso was actually the son of the local police chief Damian Davrichewy, which made the drunken Beso crazy with jealousy. Stalin himself later claimed that his father was explorer Nikolai Przhevalsky or even the future Tsar Alexander III. But Przhevalsky was homosexual and the tsarevich did not stay at the palace in Tiflis – modern-day Tbilisi, capital of Georgia – at the time when Keke was working as a maid there. On another occasion he claimed that he was the son of a priest, Charkviani perhaps. It was not impossible because the macho culture of Georgia was such that a man was expected to keep a

In 2010, this statue in Gori was pulled down at night to avoid protests by members of the local Stalin cult

mistress and Gori's priests were notoriously debauched. And on one occasion Keke let it slip that Soso's father might be his godfather, Yakov 'Koba' Egnatashvili, who supported the family.

Soso despised Beso, who thrashed him unmercifully. When he heard his father's drunken singing in the streets, he would run to a neighbour's house, where he would stay until the bully had gone to sleep. At other times his eyes would fill with tears, his lips would turn blue and he would beg his mother to hide him.

'Where's Keke's little bastard?' Beso would taunt. 'Hiding under the bed?'

Once Beso flung Soso to the floor so hard that there was blood in the child's urine for days.

'Undeserved beatings made the boy as hard and heartless as the father himself,' said schoolmate Josef Iremashvili.

It should be noted that Hitler, Stalin's soulmate, was beaten by an alcoholic father too.

When Keke tried to defend her child, she too would be beaten. Once Soso arrived at police chief Davrichewy's house covered in blood.

'Come quickly,' he said. 'He's killing my mother.'

The policeman ran to the Dzhugashvilis' house, where he found Beso strangling Keke. On another occasion, Soso tried to defend his mother himself by throwing a knife at his ravening father. Even so, his mother used to thrash him too. Although she said it did not do him any harm it left him emotionally cold. He shunned his illegitimate children and was cold and brutal with the legitimate ones. It could be said he was at least partly to blame for the deaths of both of his wives.

GEORGIA

Georgia lies in the Transcaucasus, between the Black Sea and the Caspian Sea. At the time of Stalin's birth Russia straddled Georgia's northern border and the Ottoman empire and Persia lay to the south. The medieval kingdom of Georgia was destroyed by the onslaught of the Mongols from the 13th to the 15th centuries and it was then ravaged by the Ottoman Turks and the Persians. Then in the 19th century it was gradually incorporated into the growing Russian empire.

The Georgian language is totally distinct from Russian. It has its own separate script and it enjoys a literary tradition that dates back to the 5th century AD.

When Alexander III took over the throne from his father, Alexander II, who was assassinated in 1881, he decreed that all teaching must take place in Russian. Furthermore, it was forbidden to use the Georgian language in schools.

Seizing the opportunity of the Russian Revolution, Georgia established its independence in 1917. However, Stalin ordered the Red Army to invade in 1921, after which Georgia remained part of the USSR until its collapse in 1991. As an independent state once more, Georgia has come into conflict with Russia over the breakaway republics of Abkhazia and South Ossetia.

Nevertheless, Stalin seems to have regarded his father with affection, even pride, in later life. For instance, he used the name Besoshvili – 'son of Beso' – as an alias, and his closest friends from Gori called him 'Beso'. He also claimed to have inherited his head for wine from his father, who had fed him wine from his fingertips. His own children were subjected to the same treatment, much to the annoyance of their mother. When he was in power he wrote about an anonymous shoemaker with a small workshop who was destroyed by capitalism, and he bragged that his father could make two pairs of shoes in a day.

Thanks to Beso's alcoholism the family lost their humble home, moving at least nine times. As Beso simply could not stop drinking, Keke and Soso eventually moved in with Father Charkviani. Soso then became withdrawn. He did not go out to play with the other children, insisting that he wanted to learn to read instead. His mother wanted to send him to school, but Beso was determined to turn him into a shoemaker. Then Soso was struck down with smallpox, which left him with a pockmarked face. Later on the Okhranka, or Tsarist secret police, used this as a means of identifying him. They called him 'Chopura', which means 'pockmarked'.

Schooldays

When Soso was ten years old his father's business failed. Beso lost everything and 'became a proletarian', Stalin would boast, but at the time he was devastated. Still keen to educate the child, Keke seized her opportunity. Father Charkviani asked his teenage sons to teach Soso Russian and the Davrichewys let him share their sons' lessons. Keke wanted Soso to go to the church school in Gori, but it was only open to the sons of the clergy. Father Charkviani solved the problem by telling the authorities that Soso was the son of a priest, which might have started the rumour that he was Stalin's father.

Beso continued to be a disruptive influence. Eventually, he smashed the windows of Egnatashvili's tavern and assaulted Davrichewy, who ordered him to leave Gori. He responded by moving to Tiflis, where he got a job in a shoe factory. Meanwhile Keke worked as a laundress for Egnatashvili and she also did housework for Davrichewy. Her relationship with these men, and her earthy tongue, led to more speculation about Soso's paternity. Even Stalin would sometimes call his mother a 'whore', though she continued to mollycoddle him. Although he slept on a bed made of planks, he was remembered as the best-dressed boy in his school. But he was also known as a scrapper.

'There was hardly a day when someone had not beaten him up and sent him home crying or when he hadn't beaten someone else,' said one of Father Charkviani's sons.

Maintaining this street-fighting image led to Soso playing a game of chicken with the other boys – they would grab the axles of carriages as they sped by. One day he was brought home unconscious with a permanently damaged left arm. Later in life he blamed this injury on a sledging accident, a wrestling match or a fight over a woman in Chiatura, though some whispered that it was a birth defect. But it did not stop him fighting.

Soso's behaviour exasperated his mother, who wanted him to grow up to be a priest. Gori was a violent town and Soso threw himself wholeheartedly into its gang warfare. Armed with a knife, a catapult and a home-made bow, he became a street urchin who stole apples from Prince Amilakhvari's orchards, shot an ox in the head and pushed boys who could not swim into the fast-running Kura river. Unable to dance himself, he dead-legged a boy who could dance well. He took on boys who were older and stronger, defied gang leaders and changed his allegiance whenever he felt like it. Once out of sight of his mother he had to be a leader himself and he wreaked vengeance on anyone who resembled his father.

Because Georgian had been banned in all of the schools, Soso was taught in Russian, a language he did not speak well, which would serve him well in the life he was to lead. A devout Christian, he became a choirboy, rarely missed mass and often read the psalms in church. He painted, acted, wrote poetry and generally excelled at school. When he was on class duty, he marked down anyone who cheated in a test or arrived late, which earned him the nickname 'the Gendarme'.

But he also challenged authority, because he refused to report anyone for speaking Georgian and he even threatened to kill a teacher who sought to enforce the Russian-only rule.

At the age of 12 Soso was run over by a carriage. His legs were damaged so badly that he had to be taken to the local hospital. After this experience he developed an awkward gait, which led people to call him 'the Loper' (later 'the Staggerer'). While he was still being treated, his father kidnapped him and enrolled him as an apprentice at the shoe factory where he worked. That was Stalin's only experience of proletarian labour.

After a matter of months Keke prevailed and Soso returned to school, but Beso retaliated by cutting off his support. Keke was forced to take another job to pay the school fees, although the school helped with a scholarship. However, Soso then met another obstacle when he was struck down with pneumonia, which took him to the brink of death.

Stalin in 1894 at the age of 15 when he was a pupil of the seminary in Tiflis. He could not afford the fees until a local aristocrat, Princess Baratov, helped him out

When he recovered, he repaid the school and those who had looked after him with almost daily rebellion. At the peak of his activities, he organized a protest against the school inspector that almost led to a riot. Nevertheless, Soso was intent on becoming a priest so that he could help the poor. After he had read Darwin's *On the Origin of Species*, however, he began to doubt the existence of God. Meanwhile, he fell in love with Father Charkviani's daughter.

One day, Soso climbed a tree to watch the execution of three peasants who had stolen a cow and killed a policeman. To Soso and his friends the thieves were Robin Hood figures who had flung off the oppression of the landowners. They were brave Caucasians who had been rebelling against the Russians. Their ringleader was nonchalant as he stood smiling and joking with the crowd while sympathizers threw stones at the hangman. The rope broke when the moment came, so a second attempt was made. He died this time, but only after an agonizing struggle.

The Tiflis Seminary

When Soso was 15 years old a strike almost put paid to his enrolment in the seminary at Tiflis, but again his doting mother pulled strings. Keke could barely afford the fees, but a local aristocrat, Princess Baratov, helped out. At first, Keke moved into the seminary with him, where she sewed and helped out with the catering. Soso was eventually parted from his mother, but he

Prince Ilia Chavchavadze chose five of Stalin's poems for publication in a newspaper – they were filled with violence, alienation, paranoia and murder

wrote regularly and she slept with his letters pressed to her heart.

Bullying and buggery was rife in the seminary dormitory and discipline was harsh, but there was a history of rebellion at the Stone Sack, as the seminary was known. A pupil had beaten up the rector for saying that Georgian was a 'dog's language' and in the following year the unfortunate master was found dead, slain with a traditional Georgian sword.

Soso soon became a moody romantic poet. He constantly begged the rector for help with his fees and he sang in the choir to earn a little extra cash. When his father came round to cadge drinking money, Soso threatened to have him thrown out. Beso was now, perhaps, the only true proletarian Soso knew and he had no compunction in setting the authorities on him. However, he secretly stayed in touch with his father, who later

In 1933, Osip Mandelstam made the mistake of mocking Stalin in the famous 'Stalin Epigram' and paid the price

gave him a pair of boots he had made. Stalin's love of boots stayed with him throughout his life.

During the holiday periods, Soso would go home to Gori to visit his mother. Though he was growing a beard, he still needed to snuggle up to her like a little boy. At the end of his first year at the seminary, five of his poems – in Georgian – were selected by the country's leading poet Prince Ilia Chavchavadze for publication in a newspaper. Appearing under the pen-name 'Soselo', they were filled with dark images of violence, alienation, paranoia, conspiracy and murder. It is all the more ironic that Stalin ruthlessly persecuted poets and writers when he came to power – out of jealousy, perhaps. Stalin was certainly not the simple, uncultured peasant he made himself out to be. He knew the works of Pushkin and other Russian poets by heart, he had read Shakespeare and Goethe in translation and he could recite chunks of Walt Whitman. However, his strong suit was the Georgian poets he had emulated as a youth. Like Chavchavadze, most of them advocated Georgian independence – a state of affairs that Stalin, once in power, would never countenance. One of his poems was dedicated to the poet Prince Raphael Eristavi. If any of his colleagues had dedicated a poem to a prince in their youth, it would have been used against them in the purges of the 1930s. Under Stalin, being a poet could be a dangerous profession. After writing several poems glorifying the Red Tsar, the poet Osip Mandelstam had the temerity to mock Stalin in verse. He was arrested and later died in the Gulag. Prince Ilia Chavchavadze was murdered by the Bolsheviks in 1907.

A friend in the seminary named Said Devdariani encouraged Soso to join a secret circle that met to read socialist books and other forbidden works. However, Soso was given a prolonged stay in the punishment cells after being caught reading Victor Hugo's *Ninety-Three* – a book whose hero is a priest and a revolutionary,

KARL MARX (1818–83)
AND FRIEDRICH ENGELS (1820–95)

The son of a Jewish lawyer who converted to Christianity, Karl Marx was born in Germany. He studied law at the University of Berlin, but philosophy began to claim more of his attention and he became a devotee of Hegel's dialectic – the idea that all thing arc in a continuous process of change due to conflicts between their contradictory aspects. Aftcr launching into radical journalism, Marx came to the attention of the authorities. He sought refuge in Paris and then London, where he was supported by Engels, the German-born son of the wealthy owner of a cotton plant in Manchester. Marx [*pictured above left in 1860 with wife Jenny; Engels is with his partner Mary Burns*] and Engels collaborated on the *Manifest der kommunistischen Partei* – the *Communist Manifesto* – and *Das Kapital*, which predicted the historical inevitability of the collapse of capitalism.

However, both works concerned themselves with advanced industrialized nations, such as Britain and Germany, where there was a wealthy property-owning middle class – the bourgeoisie – who benefited from the toil of a large dispossessed working class – the proletariat. Marx and Engels did not envisage a Communist revolution in countries such as Russia or China, where industrialization was in its infancy, because in those countries the bourgeoisie and the proletariat were limited in number. The true gulf lay between a large landowning aristocracy under an autocratic emperor and a vast peasantry. Consequently, Russian Communists believed that there would be two revolutions. In the first, the bourgeoisie would oust the aristocracy and industrialize the nation, creating a large working class, and in the second the workers would take over.

something that Stalin longed to be. He was also influenced by Nikolay Chernyshevsky's novel *What Is To Be Done?*, whose hero is a steely ascetic revolutionary. He read Zola, Maupassant, Balzac, Schiller, Plato in the original Greek, Thackeray in translation, Gogol, Chekhov and Dostoyevsky – though he could not stand Tolstoy's tub-thumping Christianity. Stalin became an atheist in his first year at the seminary, he was later to claim.

While aspiring to rectitude, honesty and other knightly virtues, Stalin was happy to 'expropriate', or steal, books – 'for the sake of the Revolution', he would later joke. He struggled to learn German and English so that he could read Marx and Engels in the original. At one point, he borrowed some of Marx's works from a friend and refused to return them, copying out passages by hand and distributing them.

In all, Soso was caught reading forbidden books on 13 occasions. He received nine warnings and spent weeks on end in the punishment cells, which only stiffened his resolve. While the Bible was open on his desk in the classroom, he had Marx or Plekhanov – a Russian Marxist who fled after the Revolution – open on his knees.

But *The Patricide*, a banned novel by the Georgian writer Alexander Kazbegi, perhaps had the greatest influence on Soso. The book's hero is Koba, a

Soviet-approved art: Stalin, the young revolutionary, inspires railway workers in the faith of Marxism

Political thinker Georgy Plekhanov argued that, if a small group of revolutionaries seized power from the tsar, you would merely be replacing one authoritarian regime with another — he never lived to see the truth of his words

Caucasian who fights the Russians for the sake of his friends and to protect Georgian womenfolk. Koba appealed to the young Stalin because of his thirst for vengeance, his espousal of Georgian knightly ideals and his simplistic moral code of honesty and loyalty.

'Koba became Soso's god and gave his life meaning,' said a schoolfriend. 'He wished to be Koba. He called himself "Koba" and insisted we call him that. His face shone with pride and pleasure when we called him that.'

Although Koba wreaks his vengeance on a village governor and the Russians in the novel, the book's title *The Patricide* means 'a person who kills their father'. That is exactly what Stalin wanted to do.

GEORGY VALENTINOVICH PLEKHANOV (1856–1918)

Born into a family of minor gentry, Plekhanov trained as a soldier and then studied mining before devoting himself entirely to the Populist revolutionary movement, which organized urban factory workers. In 1877, he became leader of *Zemlya i volya* or 'Land and Liberty', but three years later he went to Geneva in order to avoid being arrested. There he condemned Populism and laid down the ideological basis of Russian Marxism. Vladimir Ilich Lenin became one of his followers.

In 1883 Plekhanov founded the Liberation of Labour, which later became the Russian Social-Democratic Workers' Party. When an ideological clash led to a split, Plekhanov initially supported Lenin's Bolsheviks but then joined the Mensheviks before trying in vain to reunite the Party. The Russian Revolution of 1905 defied his 'two revolutions' theory – that there would be a bourgeois revolution followed by a proletarian one. He supported Russia in the First World War, fearing that German militarism would crush the progressive workers' movement and he greeted the February 1917 coup as the bourgeois revolution. However, when the Bolsheviks seized power, he was condemned as an 'enemy of the people'. He left Russia and died of tuberculosis soon afterwards.

CHAPTER THREE

THE SABOTEUR

By the 1890s the young Stalin was a committed Marxist. He began to put his revolutionary ideas into action by means of a campaign of arson, sabotage and strikes, and he led unarmed workers into violent confrontations with the Cossacks. After falling under the spell of another bloodthirsty revolutionary named Vladimir Ilich Lenin, he also began to learn the ruthless art of undermining his political rivals.

THE POLITICALLY MOTIVATED KOBA URGED THE SECRET CIRCLE AT THE SEMINARY TO TAKE MORE AGGRESSIVE ACTION. He already believed that the struggle to end oppression demanded conflict and death – or 'many storms, many torrents of blood', as he put it. When Seit Devdariani – the friend who introduced him in the first place – opposed him, Koba began creating a group of his own. The circle then broke into two factions – those who were for Koba and those who were against him. Koba already saw himself as a natural leader and he would not tolerate any criticism.

He cultivated radical friends including Lado Ketskhoveli, who had been arrested after being expelled from the seminaries in Tiflis and Kiev, and Silibistro 'Silva' Jibladze, who had beaten up the rector of the Tiflis seminary. Jibladze, Noe Jordania, a nobleman, and some others had founded the Georgian

A member of the Russian Social-Democratic Workers' Party, which gave birth to the Bolsheviks and Mensheviks

Socialist Party, which then took over the Marxist newspaper *Kvali* (Plough) in order to stir up revolution among the workers. Although the newspaper published Koba's poem 'Old Ninika', Jordania then rashly advised the 17-year-old seminarian to spend more time at his studies. Incensed, Koba wrote a letter denouncing Jordania, which he submitted to *Kvali*. Understandably, the newspaper refused to print the missive, so Koba then held secret meetings with some of the Marxist cells in the Tiflis seminary, in which he attacked the editorial staff at *Kvali* – handwritten accounts of the meetings were later circulated within the educational establishment. Soon Koba came to the attention of the secret police, because he was seen as a danger to the new tsar, Nicholas II. Then in August 1898, while still a teenager, Koba joined the newly formed Russian Social-Democratic Workers' Party, which would one day become the Bolshevik party.

The Party sought to bring all of the revolutionary factions together under the Marxist banner. It rejected the Populist idea that a socialist state could be built on the basis of the peasant commune, or *mir*, and insisted that Russia must first go through the capitalist stage by developing a bourgeois society with an urban proletariat as Marx had laid down. Most of the leaders were arrested after the first Party congress. In 1903 the second Party congress began in Brussels and then moved to London, after the Belgian police took an undue interest. It then split into two factions – the Bolshevik or 'majority' group under Vladimir Ilich Lenin argued that the membership should be restricted to professional revolutionaries who would be the 'vanguard of the proletariat', while the Menshevik or 'minority' wing under Yuly Martov advocated a mass movement modelled on western European social-democratic parties.

During the unsuccessful Russian Revolution of 1905, Leon Trotsky, then a Menshevik, was elected head of the St Petersburg Soviet, or council. However, it was

TSAR NICHOLAS II (1868–1918)

The last of the Romanov tsars, whose dynasty had ruled Russia since 1613, Nikolay Aleksandrovich Romanov succeeded his father Alexander III in 1894. He was crowned Tsar Nicholas II in 1896 in Moscow, the traditional seat of the Romanovs, even though the capital of Russia had been moved to St Petersburg in 1712. Sadly, the new tsar was not fitted for the task of ruling a vast empire and he is thought to have been largely responsible for Russia's humiliating defeat in the Russo-Japanese War of 1904–5. Following this debacle, he was forced into setting up a parliament, or Duma, though its powers and

its franchise were progressively restricted.

Nicholas was devoted to his wife Alexandra. However, she fell under the sway of the charismatic religious charlatan Rasputin after the mystic claimed that he could heal the royal couple's haemophiliac son Alexei. This so damaged the standing of the monarchy that many did not feel that Alexandra was fit to be left in charge when Nicholas went to the front during the Second World War. Nicholas turned out to be an inept military commander and the Russian army suffered a number of defeats at the hands of the Germans. Rioting then broke out in St Petersburg and on 8 March (23 February Old Style) 1917, Nicholas was forced to abdicate. The royal family was arrested and in April 1918 its members were shipped to Yekaterinburg in the Urals, where they were imprisoned until 17 July. At that point their captors became concerned that they would be rescued by the approaching anti-Bolshevik 'White' Russian forces so the whole family, including the children and the servants, was slaughtered in the cellar of the house in which it had been held.

the Bolsheviks who took the leading role in the October Revolution of 1917. The Bolsheviks became the Russian Communist Party (Bolsheviks) in 1918, while the Mensheviks were ruthlessly suppressed during the Russian Civil War (1918–21). In 1925, the Party was renamed the All-Union Communist Party (Bolsheviks) and in 1952 it finally became the Communist Party of the Soviet Union.

Koba now avoided going home to see his mother. Instead he took work as a private tutor, though he spent his time trying to convert his pupils to Marxism. Sometimes he would entertain them by mimicking the peasants he saw in the countryside. On one occasion, while visiting a church, he persuaded a pupil to smash up an old icon and urinate on it.

At the seminary he became increasingly rebellious. Keke grew worried and went to visit him but he hugged her and told her that he was not a rebel.

'It was his first lie,' she said later.

But then he began to fight with his teachers, many of whom would later end up in his jails, and he was eventually expelled in May 1899, possibly for fathering an illegitimate child whose mother he had abandoned. He left behind him unpaid school fees and an unsettled bill for books he had stolen from the seminary's library. Although he had not qualified as a priest, the seminary had given him a classical education, turned him into an atheist and a Marxist, and made him familiar with all of the tools of repression that he would later skilfully deploy. Soon afterwards, the members of Koba's inner circle of Marxist seminarians were expelled too, which gave rise to the rumour that he had betrayed them to the Okhranka. The Okhranka – or 'Okhrana' as it is called in English – was the tsarist secret police force that was founded to combat political terrorism and revolutionary activity. Its agents were particularly active following the unsuccessful Russian Revolution of 1905, when they infiltrated trade unions, political parties and radical newspapers. Aided by a Special Corps of Gendarmes, they are thought to have used torture, even though it had been outlawed in Russia in the early 19th century.

It was frequently alleged that Stalin worked for the Okhranka and that he used it to rid himself of his political rivals. Others say, more charitably, that his links with the Okhranka were through double agents inside the organization. The Okhranka was abolished after the February Revolution in 1917, but its methods were adopted by the Cheka, the NKVD, the MGB, the MVD, the KGB and other secret police forces under the Bolsheviks.

The Rise of Lenin

So by 1899 Koba had fallen out with the other radicals in Tiflis and he could not go home to his mother, who was angry with him for being expelled from the seminary. It was at this stage that he fell under the spell of a new radical thinker, who used the pseudonym 'Tulin'. This was Vladimir Ilich Ulyanov, who was later known as Lenin.

VLADIMIR ILICH LENIN (1870–1924)

Vladimir Ilich Ulyanov, later Lenin, was born into a well-educated and cultured family. He trained to become a lawyer but by the time he was admitted to the bar in Samara, on the eastern bank of the Volga, he was already a dedicated revolutionary. It was a family trait because in 1887 his elder brother had been hanged for conspiring to assassinate Tsar Alexander III. Expelled from his university as a result of his activities, Lenin [*far right in family grouping*] became a Marxist after reading *Das Kapital*. He still qualified as a lawyer, however, and in 1893 he moved to St Petersburg so that he could work as a public defender while mixing in Marxist circles. Two years later he was sent abroad to make contact with exiled Marxists, notably Georgy Plekhanov, and on his return he formed the Union for the Struggle for the Liberation of the Working Class with Yuly Martov, who became the leader of the Mensheviks. However, the two revolutionaries were arrested and exiled to Siberia. During his banishment Lenin married fellow political exile Nadezhda Krupskaya, and he adopted the name Lenin – a possible reference to the Siberian river Lena.

In 1902 Lenin published the pamphlet *What Is To Be Done?*, which argued that the proletariat would not spontaneously rise up and destroy capitalism. What was needed, Lenin wrote, was a vanguard of highly disciplined revolutionaries and he worked tirelessly towards that end.

Lenin's great opportunity came in February 1917, when the tsar was deposed

by war-weary Russian workers and soldiers. Kaiser Wilhelm II feared the Communists as much as the Russian tsar, but he nevertheless allowed Lenin and his lieutenants to pass through Germany in a sealed train in the hope that the return of these revolutionary socialists would undermine the Russian war effort. His plan succeeded brilliantly. In November 1917 Lenin's Bolsheviks seized power from the Provisional Government led by moderate socialist Aleksandr Kerensky. Lenin had dreamt of provoking a worldwide revolution in which workers would throw off their capitalist shackles, but now he concentrated his efforts on the newly founded Soviet Union, where he developed the most brutal tactics as a means of holding on to power, thereby paving the way for the dictatorship of Joseph Stalin. He already foresaw the Party being torn apart by the rivalry of such powerful personalities as Stalin and Trotsky, but while he criticized Trotsky, he recommended that Stalin be removed from his post as general secretary. But there was nothing he could do about it because he died of a stroke on the morning of 21 January 1924.

Writing in his new newspaper *Iskra* (Spark), Lenin propagated the idea of a revolutionary party led by a tiny militant elite. Koba vowed to meet him at all costs. He was now a committed revolutionary.

Koba the Revolutionary

Even Marxist revolutionaries need to support themselves, so Koba took a job as a meteorologist at Tiflis Observatory. Meanwhile, Koba joined his revolutionary comrade Lado Ketskhoveli in organizing a strike that paralyzed the tram system in Tiflis. Koba was arrested early in 1900, after which he continued to work with Ketskhoveli, who was later shot dead by a prison guard. Nicknamed 'the Priest' because of his proselytizing zeal, Koba agitated among the railway workers and then addressed a secret May Day rally, where the attendees sang the *Marseillaise* and organized a strike that lost his father his job at the shoe factory. It was their last contact.

Koba now prepared a reading list of 300 titles for his circle and for extra money he took in pupils, teaching them Russian and Marxism for ten kopecks an hour. One of them was Kamo Ter-Petrossian, a would-be soldier who became one of Stalin's most murderous henchmen.

Even at drunken parties Koba could be found devouring books.

'What are you reading?' he was asked on one occasion.

'Napoleon Bonaparte's *Memoirs*,' he replied. 'It's amazing what mistakes he made. I'm making a note of them.'

Although Koba spent as much time attacking moderate Marxists as he did attacking the state he became a target of the secret police, which forced him to live underground at the expense of friends and Party comrades, who were expected to put him up. In 1901 Koba even managed to organize a May Day demonstration while he was moving from place to place, though it was put down by sabre-wielding policemen and Cossacks on horseback. Fourteen workers were seriously wounded and 50 more were arrested, while the newspaper *Kvali* was closed down and its proprietor, Jordania, was arrested. Meanwhile Koba fled back to Gori. Stalin later considered this May Day demonstration to be his first success.

Next he sought to bring the railway workers out on strike. The first move in his campaign was to have the railway director, Vedenev, shot dead. Now using the pseudonym 'David', Koba had taken to heart the message of *The Revolutionary*

This stamp shows Stalin's insistence that he be recognized as the natural successor to Marx, Engels and Lenin

SIMON 'KAMO' TER-PETROSSIAN (1882–1922)

A Georgian Bolshevik of Armenian descent, Kamo Ter-Petrossian was Stalin's early protégé. The two grew up together in Gori, where Soso encouraged him to read and converted him to Marxism. Kamo earned his nickname from Soso because he kept mispronouncing the word *komu* – meaning 'to whom' – as 'kamo', while he was trying to learn Russian.

Kamo was a psychopath who became Koba's willing executioner, often begging him to order a hit. On one occasion he tore open a man's chest and ripped his heart out. A master of disguise, he was as convincing a prince as he was a laundrywoman. He led the robberies that Stalin planned, often with reckless courage, and even Lenin admired him, calling him the 'Caucasian bandit'. In May 1907 a bomb blew up in his face while he was setting the fuse, but although he lost an eye he recovered sufficiently to lead the daring robbery that took place in Yerevan Square (now Freedom Square) in Tiflis on 12 June 1907. Having achieved his object of raising funds for the Bolshevik cause, Kamo took the money to Lenin in Finland.

After being arrested in Berlin, Kamo pretended to be insane in order to avoid being sent back to Russia. Despite being tortured he managed to convince the German doctors, but he was extradited all the same. Back in Russia, he continued playing the part of a madman while he was being tried for the Tiflis robbery and once again he was put to the test by being tortured. The Russian doctors who examined him were also satisfied that he was deranged, so he escaped the gallows. Instead, he was sent to Metekhi castle, where there was a unit for the criminally insane. In August 1912 he sawed through his shackles and the bars of his cell and made his escape before fleeing to Paris to see Lenin.

Irrepressible as ever, Kamo had surgery performed on his eye and then he returned to Koba's side in Tiflis, where they pulled off another daring robbery. He was once again caught and this time he was given four death sentences – but luck was on his side, because Nicholas II had decided to celebrate the 300th anniversary of the Romanov dynasty by announcing an amnesty.

Instead, his death sentence was commuted to 20 years' imprisonment. However, he was liberated by the 1917 Revolution only five years later.

During the Russian Civil War, Kamo became Stalin's devoted – and bloodthirsty – lieutenant. He would test his men by putting them in front of a firing squad – if any of them pleaded for their lives he would shoot them.

'That way you could be absolutely sure they won't let you down,' he said.

Kamo was finally killed when he was run over by a truck while cycling home. He had just begun writing his memoirs, which gave an account of Stalin's involvement in the Tiflis bank robbery. The fact that the only bicycle in Tiflis should be hit by the only truck was seen as something of a joke at the time.

Tsarist police disperse Obukhov factory workers taking part in a May Day demonstration in St Petersburg, 1901. These protests are viewed historically as a rehearsal for the strikes which followed in 1905

Catechism of the nihilist Sergey Nechayev, who wrote in 1869: 'All tender feeling for family, friendship, love, gratitude and even honour must be squashed by the sole passion for revolutionary work.'

It was clear to Koba that violent action now needed to be taken without compunction against anyone who might report him to the Okhranka, who were on his trail. As the secret police closed in, Koba was sent to the Black Sea oil port of Batumi by the Party, whose members had now learnt to fear him. Batumi was a boom town which boasted a cricket ground and an English yacht club. Koba scored some notable successes in his first three months there. The Rothschild oil refinery burned down on the day after he got a job there, there was a strike, horses belonging to would-be blacklegs were slaughtered and the prison was stormed to free jailed comrades. Then Koba ordered the crowd to advance on the gathered Cossacks. Thirteen died and 54 others were wounded, which left Koba exhilarated.

'Today we advanced several years,' he said. He considered that the political value of his actions outweighed any human cost.

He flooded the town with Marxist pamphlets and brought a new aggressive spirit to the local party, who considered him an intellectual after he plied them with Gogol. They too nicknamed him 'the Priest'. But he had far from priestly habits. He became embroiled in an affair with a married woman named Natasha Kirtava and when the presses printing his pamphlets broke down he sent his henchmen out to steal spare parts. However, his ruthless methods alienated many. He spent his time sniffing out police informers and anyone he suspected was killed. Von Stein, the Rothschilds' manager, was also assassinated on his orders. The actual murders would be carried out by his henchmen, who dubbed themselves 'Sosoists'. 'God forbid we die in our beds,' became his slogan.

Constantly sought by the police, he once hid beneath the voluminous skirts of a female comrade to avoid arrest. On another occasion he donned a dress himself and escaped disguised as a woman. Later on he and the typesetters who printed his pamphlets dressed as Muslim women with their faces covered by veils. But despite his disguises, Koba was soon caught and imprisoned. Under interrogation, he claimed that he was with his mother in Gori at the time of the Cossack massacre. He wrote her a note asking her to support his alibi but when a schoolmate, Josef Iremashvili, tried to deliver it the message was intercepted. As a result, Iremashvili, Keke and her brother, Koba's uncle, were arrested. She was then berated by Beso. If she had not sent him to school, he said, Koba would now be a craftsman rather than a jailbird. But, like a true revolutionary, Koba cared little about Keke's sufferings.

'We didn't have much time for our mothers,' he said.

Another intercepted note resulted in the arrest of Koba's former pupil, Giorgi Elisabedashvili, who soon joined him in the jail at Batumi. Koba's girlfriend Natasha Kirtava was taken there too. They were impressed by how quickly Koba asserted power in prison. He suborned guards, bullied friends and turned his back on

Batumi on the Black Sea coast was a boom town, which boasted a cricket pitch and an English yacht club. Stalin's activities meant he had to forgo the pleasures of the seaside when he was imprisoned on suspicion of inciting rebellion

Mugshots of Stalin held by the Okhranka (the tsarist secret police) in St Petersburg. Stalin was devoted to the overthrow of the authorities, but his role as a double agent gave him cover for anything he got up to

comrades in favour of criminals. Fellow intellectuals, he said, were to be considered rats who should be killed. He continued to run the local Party from his cell and he also studied German and economic theory, reading the *Communist Manifesto* aloud for the edification of prisoners and guards alike.

In March 1902 a new essay was doing the rounds. It was *What Is To Be Done? Burning Questions of our Movement*, by the Marxist now calling himself Lenin. It called for a new vanguard of ruthless conspirators to lead the Russian Social-Democratic Workers' Party. Like Stalin, Lenin wanted to exclude the workers while ruling in their name and at the Second Congress in 1903 his majority faction – the Bolsheviks – restricted Party membership to professional revolutionaries, while the minority faction – the Mensheviks – argued for the inclusion of the masses. Stalin was an instant Bolshevik, said Iremashvili.

YULY MARTOV (1873–1923)

Born Yuly Osipovich Zederbaum to middle-class parents, Yuly Martov was a member of the Bund, a Jewish socialist group. In 1895 he and Lenin formed the St Petersburg-based Union of Struggle for the Liberation of the Working Class. He was arrested and exiled for three years in 1897 and then he joined Lenin in Switzerland as editor of *Iskra*.

In 1903, the two fell out and Martov became leader of the Mensheviks. During the First World War he called for peace without victory and after the October Revolution he opposed the Bolsheviks' dictatorial methods. Leaving the Soviet Union in 1920, he spent the rest of his life editing the *Socialist Courier* in Berlin.

There was not enough evidence to charge Koba with leading the Batumi riots, but he was also being investigated for his activities in Tiflis. Looking for a way out, he used his influence to get himself transferred to the prison hospital. Then, against Communist convention, he made three separate appeals to the governor-general of the Caucasus, Prince Golitsyn, claiming that he needed to look after his aged mother. All was in vain, however, because a violent protest against the visit of the Exarch (archbishop) of Georgia led to his transfer to a tougher prison, Kutaisi, in western Georgia. When Natasha was sent with him he demanded that a carriage be provided to take them to the station.

Once installed in his new prison he organized a noisy protest, which forced the governor to have the prison surrounded by troops. Koba was then sentenced to three years' exile in Siberia, but it took the authorities six weeks to locate him. It is thought that this was because of the rivalry between the Okhranka and the tsar's semi-military political police, the Gendarmes. Because Koba was a double agent, the two organizations could well have been hiding him from each other.

Ruthless as he was, Koba could also be squeamish. On the way to Siberia, one of his fellow prisoners had to have his gangrenous leg amputated. Koba would not help hold the man down and he could not even bear to watch the operation. However, that did not stop him getting into a fight with a criminal over a tobacco pouch. His ribs were broken and he was knocked out.

'As I was coming round, it occurred to me that politicians must always win over allies,' he said.

Having developed toothache at this point he unwisely tried to cure it with arsenic. Unsurprisingly, several of his teeth then fell out.

Koba's place of exile was Novaya Uda, 2,500 miles from Georgia. His fellow exiles there were three Jewish intellectuals, whom he hated. He slept on a trestle table in the larger of the two rooms that comprised a peasants' ramshackle home, while the family slept around the stove in the other one. The exiles received a small allowance from the tsar for rent and other necessities but there was little to do but read, drink and fornicate. Koba would go on pub crawls with exiled criminals. However, this was considered to be an offence under the revolutionaries' code and he was later put on trial by his puritanical comrades.

The disastrous war against Japan that had started in 1904 presented the revolutionaries with the opportunity they had craved. Koba was reading the *History of the French Revolution* at the time, which inspired him. Somehow he managed to obtain the forged ID of a police agent and after several bungled attempts he made it back to Tiflis.

Many of his old friends were not pleased to see him back, not least because he insisted on maintaining an independent Georgian Social-Democratic Party, while his comrades

THE RUSSO-JAPANESE WAR (1904–5)

In the late 19th century Russia and Japan competed for dominance in Manchuria and Korea. Although Japan had won the Sino-Japanese war of 1894–5, Russia forced China to hand over Port Arthur – now Lü-shun – and then occupied the rest of the Liaotung Peninsula in southern Manchuria. It also won the right to extend the newly constructed Trans-Siberian Railway across Manchuria to the Russian seaport of Vladivostok.

When Russia reneged on an agreement to withdraw its troops from Manchuria, the Japanese fleet launched a surprise raid on Port Arthur. At the same time, the Japanese army overran Korea and the Liaotung Peninsula before making a land attack on Port Arthur, which eventually fell to the invaders. The Japanese then won a costly victory at Mukden, now Shen-yang.

In order to maintain its command of the sea the Japanese navy attempted to contain the Russia Far Eastern fleet in Port Arthur and Vladivostok. Tsar Nicholas retaliated by despatching the Baltic fleet to the area, which lay 18,000 nautical miles from its home waters, but the Russian naval force was decisively defeated at the Battle of Tsushima. However, Japan was now financially exhausted and there was unrest in Russia, so the two sides met at the negotiating table. Under the mediation of President Theodore Roosevelt, a peace treaty was concluded in Portsmouth, New Hampshire, in which Russia conceded much of Manchuria and recognized Japan's control of Korea.

The Russo-Japanese War was not just a military disaster for Russia, but it also revealed the shortcomings of the country's ruling elite who were mired in the past and blind to the country's social and economic problems

had converted to Marxist Internationalism. 'Marx is an ass. What he wrote should be written as I say,' he yelled, storming out of one meeting.

He was then forced to undergo a Marxist re-education programme – or face expulsion from the Party. Eventually he wrote a credo that renounced his heretical views and he was exonerated when it was published. Later Stalin sought out copies and had them destroyed – many of those who read it were later shot. Meanwhile he ceaselessly sponged off others, telling them that they owed him a living because he was on a sacred mission.

Again, some of those who helped him were later executed. Koba slept with a number of women who helped look after him and he distributed pamphlets from brothels on the dubious reasoning that there were no police informers there. Other pamphlets were thrown from the balcony at the theatre, disrupting performances.

Koba was no more popular when he returned to Batumi, this time disguised in an ornate soldier's uniform. Natasha Kirtava was threatened with expulsion from the

Party if she put him up but she eventually gave him the money to get back to Tiflis. He was angry when she refused to join him. When he returned to Batumi at a later date he was beaten up.

As setbacks in the Russo-Japanese war sent the country into chaos, Koba played hide and seek with the police force. Meanwhile, he spent his time defaming the Mensheviks in western Georgia where he travelled with a fishing rod, pretending to be an angler. His purge of the Mensheviks from local Party committees brought him to the attention of Lenin.

Koba then disrupted a meeting that was calling for the tsar to write a constitution, because he despised such bourgeois liberalism. However, on Sunday 9 January 1905 – Bloody Sunday – a similar demand for a constitution resulted in carnage. While a group of workers were carrying their petition to the Winter Palace in St Petersburg they were fired on by the army. Over a hundred were killed and there were strikes and uprisings across the country.

Tsarist police and soldiers prepare to disperse workers marching on the Winter Palace to present a petition to Tsar Nicholas II. Over a hundred demonstrators were killed as the Imperial Guard fired indiscriminately into the crowd

CHAPTER FOUR

THE GANGSTER

During the Russian Revolution of 1905, a general strike and the formation of Soviets (workers' councils) had forced the tsar into establishing a legislative assembly (Duma) before making fundamental reforms. But these concessions were not good enough for the Bolsheviks, who wanted a workers' revolution. In order to fund the Party until it achieved its goals, Stalin turned to robbery, piracy, blackmail, extortion, kidnapping and racketeering.

Baku used to be the world centre of oil production. Above can be seen the dangerous and damaging oil lakes owned by the Nobel family. In those days, fires were a constant danger and social conflagration was never far away

O N 9 JANUARY 1905, BLOODY SUNDAY, COMRADE KOBA WAS IN OIL-RICH BAKU, WHICH HAD LONG BEEN A CENTRE OF BOLSHEVIK AGITATION. A little later, on 6 February, some Armenians shot an Azeri Turk, who was then known as a Tartar. Incensed, the Tartars fought back, killing all the Armenians they could find. While the rest of the empire was indulging itself in one of its periodic anti-Semitic pogroms, Baku was involved in its own race war, in which over 2,000 people died.

The 1905 Revolution

Koba responded by forming the Bolshevik Battle Squad. Largely made up of Muslims, its ostensible aim was to separate the two warring communities, but in reality it used the ensuing disorder to steal any printing equipment it could find. It also raised money for the Party by running protection rackets. After informing them that they were in danger, Koba took money from the Armenian merchants on the understanding that they would be conveyed to safety in the countryside. Meanwhile, he agitated against the Mensheviks in Tiflis and across Georgia. Often his invective turned to blatant anti-Semitism, because many of the leading Mensheviks were Jews. While the Mensheviks favoured government reforms, Koba advocated armed resistance. He pursued his aim by setting up terrorist Red Battle Squads across Georgia.

The wealthy manganese mining town of Chiatura became a bastion of Bolshevism. There Koba organized a squad of gangsters who robbed banks, ambushed Cossacks, disarmed soldiers and murdered policemen and informers. The mine owners also made their contribution to Party funds because their managers would be murdered and their mines blown up if they refused. At the same time, Koba protected them from being robbed by common or garden thieves. He finally assumed total control in Chiatura by taking over the newspapers and assassinating the members of the police force one by one. The Mensheviks were still in control in the rest of Georgia but Koba fought them viciously.

'Against them,' he said, 'any methods are fine.'

By the end of May 1905, the Japanese had defeated Russia on land and at sea. A new liberal viceroy was sent to Tiflis, but Georgia was so lawless that he had to declare martial law. However, the Red chieftain known as 'Koba of Gori' was beyond his reach, because Chiatura nestled in the hills of northern Imereti. But inaccessibility had its price because Koba had to ferry ammunition, money and printing presses over the mountains by donkey. Along the way he sang and recited poetry.

As the tsarist autocracy in St Petersburg teetered, 'Soviets of Workers' Deputies' were set up across the country. Delegates from each town's factories and workshops would form a committee that organized strike actions and kept up basic municipal services during the crisis. In October, a general strike was called and a Soviet was set up in St Petersburg under Leon Trotsky. This one was different from the rest, because

Chiatura lies along the Kvirila river in the foothills of the Caucasus and it was from here that Stalin sent his Bolshevik militias out across Georgia — owners of the manganese mines in the area were expected to contribute to his war chest

The First Council of Workers, Peasants and Soldiers' Deputies, 1917: the organization of workers' soviets in pro Revolutionary Russia laid the foundations for what was to come when the tsar was toppled from power

it claimed to be an alternative government. Ex-finance minister Sergei Witte, who had just concluded peace negotiations with Japan, recommended that the government should agree to the demands of the liberals and create an elected legislative assembly. Meanwhile, Koba was closing his grip back in Tiflis. He absolutely insisted that his henchman from Gori, Josef Davrichewy, should join him, 'while there's still time'.

'If not....' Koba narrowed his eyes and left the rest unsaid.

Koba found accommodation at the workrooms of three young Georgian dressmakers, the Svanidze sisters. It thrilled him to be holding meetings with his gangsters and terrorists in one room, while the women were giving a general's wife a fitting in the next. Documents were even hidden in the mannequins. The youngest of the sisters, Ekaterina – or 'Kato' – became Koba's lover and then his first wife.

The Fight Goes On

On 17 October 1905 the tsar conceded a constitution and a parliament – the Duma – as well as a free press, but that did not end the unrest. Armed bands of monarchists called the Black Hundreds then began massacring left-wing activists, students and Jews and in Baku the oilfield was set on fire as armed Armenian nationalists, known as Dashnaks, began murdering Tartars in the surrounding

Lenin married Nadezhda Krupskaya in July 1898: there has always been speculation whether they married for love or 'for the cause'. Lenin led the Bolsheviks whose members included the ambitious Stalin

Azeri villages. Nevertheless, jubilant crowds swelled in the streets of Tiflis. Koba clambered on top of a tram and exhorted the people to make one more push to bring the throne crashing down. He denounced the Duma as 'a negation of the people's revolution'.

'Smash this trap,' he said, 'and wage a ruthless struggle against liberal enemies of the people.'

This put him, once again, at odds with the local Party. Koba's stance was clear when he addressed a local fundraising event.

'Do you think we can defeat the tsar with empty hands? Never! We need three things: one – guns, two – guns and three – more and more guns.'

To this end, he led three daring daylight raids on Tiflis's arsenals and then travelled back and forth between Tiflis and Baku, stirring up trouble and storming the jails. His men fought with the Cossacks and the Black Hundreds, but when the viceroy offered the Mensheviks guns to keep the peace Koba was nowhere to be seen. He was on his way to Finland to meet Lenin.

By the time Koba reached St Petersburg, the tsar had arrested Trotsky and other members of the Soviet and had closed down the Communist newspaper *Novaya Zhizn* (New Life). However, after two days he contacted Lenin's wife Nadezhda Krupskaya, who gave him tickets for Tammefors – now Tampere – in Finland, where the Bolshevik conference was to be held. There Koba would meet 'the mountain eagle of our Party'.

'Lenin had taken shape in my imagination as a stately and imposing giant,' Koba wrote. 'Imagine my disappointment when I saw the most ordinary man, below average height, in no way different from ordinary mortals.'

Koba was equally unimpressed when Lenin advocated the Party's participation in the elections to the Duma, but when he stood up and attacked him Lenin unexpectedly backed down. Thanks to Koba the delegates took an altogether more robust approach to revolution.

'During intervals at the conference, we learnt how to shoot,' said Nadezhda Krupskaya.

Koba was armed at all times and after growing annoyed during a debate he went outside and fired into the air.

'Among all these chatterboxes,' boasted Stalin, 'I was the only one who'd already organized and led men in combat.'

Things were moving fast in Russia. The Bolshevik militia had rebelled in Moscow, but the tsar's Semyonovsky Guards were now putting them down. Blood stained the streets of St Petersburg and the conference had broken up in disarray, so Koba returned to Georgia. On his arrival he discovered that his Battle Squads had

THE COSSACKS

The Cossacks, or *Kazaks* – which means 'adventurers' or 'free men' – originally came from north of the Caucasus between the Black Sea and the Caspian Sea. In the 15th century they were exclusively Tartars, but then other peasants fleeing from serfdom began to join them. Ferocious fighters, they were granted autonomy by the thrones of Poland and Russia in return for their military services. Most served as cavalrymen. Three regiments of Cossacks formed part of the Russian Imperial Guard, as well as the *Konvoi* – the tsar's mounted escort. During the 19th and 20th centuries the tsar used the Cossacks to put down strikes, demonstrations and other revolutionary activities, but after the October Revolution the Soviets sought to suppress them.

During the Russian Civil War they formed the core of the White Army in the south and around 30,000 of them fled Russia after their defeat.

been put down by the Cossacks, so he rapidly reformed them into a secret squad of assassins. The 'Butcher of Tiflis', General Fyodor Griiazanov, was first on Koba's hit list. His men threw home-made grenades into the general's carriage, blowing him to bits and slightly injuring Koba.

Emboldened by their success, Koba's *Druzhina*, or 'Outfit', hit a pawnshop and then embarked on a series of daring bank robberies. They held up stagecoaches and then stopped a gold train that was taking the miners' wages to Chiatura. After a shoot-out they made off with 21,000 roubles, 15,000 of which were sent to Lenin in Finland. Comrades suspected of pilfering the proceeds were brutally tortured or killed. Koba was philosophical about this.

'You can't pick a rose without pricking yourself on a thorn,' he would say. 'Leaves fall in autumn, but new ones grow in the spring.'

He planned future operations by using toy soldiers and he continued writing for the radical press under the pen-names 'Koba' and 'Besoshvili' – or 'son of Beso'. While travelling to the next congress in Berlin via Stockholm, the Caucasian delegates got drunk and began to argue, at which point Koba opposed Lenin's proposal to nationalize the land. Instead he insisted that it should be given to the peasants. But that was the altruism of youth.

When he became Stalin he would oversee a collectivization campaign that would rob the peasants of their smallholdings and result in the deaths of over ten million people. The congress also voted to end bank robberies but Lenin refused to comply – he needed the money, so he provided Koba's gang with more guns and more bombs.

Back in Tiflis, Koba married Kato Svanidze. It was a church wedding, despite his avowed atheism. Shortly afterwards, he came close to shooting a policeman who had seen him locking up his secret printing press. Fortunately for the man, Koba's brother-in-law quickly informed him that the policeman had been bribed not to interfere.

Although the Mensheviks were in the ascendancy, the Bolsheviks had the cash, thanks to Comrade Koba's heists. They became even richer when Koba turned to piracy on the Black Sea, on one occasion sinking a ship.

Afterwards he ordered the immediate murder of seven gang members on the grounds that they were

Yekaterina Svanidze was a tailor to the wives of army officers. She married Stalin in 1903 – they had a son, Yakov – and she died in 1907, the love of Stalin's life

unreliable, including four of the sailors who had collaborated with him. Their bodies were left to be eaten by jackals while he boarded the train back to Tiflis with the proceeds. Meanwhile his young wife, now heavily pregnant, had been left to fend for herself. As the wife of a known bank robber she was arrested along with her cousin,

MAKSIM MAKSIMOVICH LITVINOV (1876–1951)

Born Meir Henoch Mojszewicz Wallach-Finkelstein, aka Max Wallach, to a wealthy Jewish family in Bialystok, Litvinov [*pictured right with Trotsky at a military parade*] assumed his pseudonym when he joined the Russian Social-Democratic Workers' Party in 1898. He then enlisted in the Bolshevik faction in 1903 and, while in exile in Switzerland, he edited Lenin's newspaper *Iskra*. After the Russian Revolution of 1905, he went on to edit the Bolshevik's first legal newspaper in St Petersburg, *Novaya Zhizn*, and, following the 1917 Revolution, he became the Soviet government's representative in London. In 1929, he concluded the Litvinov Pact, a peace treaty between the Soviet Union, Poland, Romania, Latvia and Estonia, and he led the Soviet delegation to the League of Nations World Disarmament Conference in 1927–30. Then Stalin appointed him minister for foreign affairs. In 1933, he persuaded the United States to recognize the Soviet government and President Franklin Roosevelt sent Harpo Marx to Russia as a goodwill ambassador.

Following the rise of Hitler, Litvinov negotiated treaties with France and Czechoslovakia, but in 1939 he was sacked as foreign minister. The fact that he was a Jew made it difficult to negotiate a non-aggression pact with Germany. After Germany attacked the Soviet Union in 1941, Litvinov became the Soviet ambassador to the United States. On his deathbed he told his wife to return to Britain, where they had married in 1918.

The London congress of the Russian Social-Democratic Workers' Party was held in a church in Islington. It was here that Comrade Koba first met Lev Bronstein, who had already adopted his revolutionary pseudonym Leon Trotsky. Koba hated him on sight, while Trotsky dismissed the Georgians as bumpkins. It was here also that Koba decided that the Bolsheviks were true Russians, while the Mensheviks – like Trotsky – were Jews. As a result, Koba stopped writing in Georgian. From then on, he expressed himself only in Russian.

LEON TROTSKY (1879–1940)

Born Lev Davidovich Bronstein to a family of Jewish landowners, Trotsky became a Marxist at university. He helped organize the underground South Russian Workers' Union and he published pamphlets under the name 'Lvov'. In 1898 he was arrested, after which he spent two years in prison before being exiled to Siberia. In 1902, he escaped from Siberia and made his way to London using a forged passport in the name of 'Trotsky', a name he had borrowed from one of his prison guards. When he got to London he worked with Lenin on the revolutionary newspaper *Iskra*. At the second congress of the Russian Social-Democratic Workers' Party, held in Brussels and London in July 1903, he sided with the Mensheviks.

He returned to Russia during the Revolution of 1905. His intention was to lead the St Petersburg Soviet of Workers' Deputies and organize strikes, but he was once again arrested, tried and exiled. However, he managed to escape in 1907, at first settling in Vienna.

Following the outbreak of the Revolution of February 1917 Trotsky returned to St Petersburg, which had been renamed Petrograd, but he was arrested in a crack-down in July. In jail he became a Bolshevik. After the October Revolution, he became People's Commissar for Foreign Affairs and he led the peace talks with Germany at Brest-Litovsk. During the Russian Civil War he became commissar for war and was responsible for the creation of the Red Army, though his policy of recruiting former tsarist officers as 'military specialists' brought him into conflict with Stalin.

Trotsky was seen as Lenin's number two when the Russian Civil War ended. He founded the Comintern in 1919, which aimed to foster world revolution, and in 1921 he revealed his steely nature when dealing with the rebellious sailors at the Kronstadt naval base. Although they had backed the Revolution in 1917, they now rebelled against the Communist Party's dictatorship, demanding 'soviets without Bolsheviks'. Trotsky led the force that put them down, shooting or imprisoning the survivors.

When Lenin fell ill, Trotsky attacked the ruling troika of Stalin, Kamenev and Zinoviev, who responded by accusing him of factionalism. Deceived about the date of Lenin's funeral, he was not present for the great state occasion, thereby allowing Stalin to take centre-stage. In October 1926 he was expelled from the Politburo. The following year he and Zinoviev were dropped from the Central Committee and expelled from the Party. In January 1928, he was exiled to Alma Ata in Kazakhstan and a year later he was banished from the Soviet Union.

In 1936, he found refuge in Mexico, where he had an affair with the artist Frida Kahlo. During the Moscow show trials of 1936–8, he was represented, in absentia, as the principal conspirator, after which Stalin ordered his death. The deed was carried out by the Spanish Communist Ramón Mercader on 20 August 1940. After winning the confidence of the Trotsky household, Mercader pierced Trotsky's skull with an ice pick.

While Stalin was away, Pyotr Stolypin, the Russian premier, rounded up revolutionaries who he then had exiled or killed

who was sentenced to death. Kato was only released after the intervention of her sister, who was making a dress for the wife of the police chief at the time. Soon afterwards, she gave birth to a baby boy. Ostensibly a loving father, Koba was annoyed by the child's crying, which disturbed his work.

Stalin in London

Koba then headed off to meet up with Lenin in Berlin, where they planned the biggest robbery yet. The men travelled separately to London in 1907, where their arrival was reported with some excitement by the *Daily Mirror*. The newspaper paid particular attention to the gun-toting young lady revolutionaries in Koba's Outfit, with their fashionable hairstyles. But while Lenin stayed in the Imperial Hotel and then took rooms in Kensington, Koba was put up in dosshouses and cheap lodgings in Stepney and Whitechapel, though he did venture as far as Chelsea for a drinks party. On one occasion, it was only the intervention of Russian exile Maksim Litvinov that saved him from being beaten up by London dockers. When he was not tramping the streets, he passed the time in churches, where he listened to sermons in order to improve his English.

Despite Lenin's command of the congress, the Mensheviks managed to pass a resolution condemning bank robberies and they threatened to expel anyone who committed them. The Party was already short of funds so with that avenue closed the delegates had to appeal to an American soap tycoon, Joseph Fels, for the fare home. They signed a note promising to pay him back by 1 January 1908, using their aliases. Stalin's pseudonym was 'Vasily from Baku', though he was travelling under the name Koba Ivanovich. The money was only paid back to the deceased tycoon's heirs when the Party came to power in 1917.

Stalin claimed to have met Benito Mussolini – then a socialist – during his stay in London, though it is more likely that they met later in Germany. On his way back to Georgia, Koba spent a week in Paris, which was a mistake. While he was away the Russian premier, Pyotr Archad'evich Stolypin had restricted the franchise in order to ensure a conservative majority in the Duma. He then rounded up the revolutionaries, who were either deported to Siberia in 'Stolypin carriages' or hanged – the noose became known as the 'Stolypin necktie'. Koba quickly struck back. The Outfit provided the explosives that were used to blow up Stolypin's house and Stolypin was eventually shot and killed while attending an opera with the tsar in 1911.

On the Run

Although the London congress had banned bank robberies, Koba told the Bolsheviks in Tiflis that Lenin had approved his plans for a new heist. Koba's gunmen got round the ban on hold-ups by temporarily resigning from the Party. Meanwhile Stalin's poetic mentor, Prince Ilia Chavchavadze, was assassinated. It is thought that Stalin had a hand in the murder.

The big heist came on 13 June 1907, when a consignment of between 250,000 and 341,000 roubles – some £1.7 million ($2.7 million) in today's money – was being delivered to the State Bank in Tiflis. The coach carrying the money was hijacked in Yerevan Square (later Beria, then Lenin and now Freedom Square). Ten bombs were thrown, which disembowelled the horses and blew their legs off. Every pane of glass in the square was shattered and the streets were filled with blood and severed body parts. Finally Kamo and the Outfit opened fire on the police and the Cossacks who were guarding the shipment.

In the confusion Kamo seized a police carriage and made off with the money. The rest of the robbers also escaped. Forty people were killed and another 24 were seriously wounded. Three of the dead were Cossacks and the rest were bank officials or bystanders. The story appeared in newspapers as far away as London and New York. Apart from planning the robbery, it is not clear what part Koba actually played in the incident. When he came to power Stalin remained silent about the episode, though a Soviet hagiographer claimed that he had been injured while throwing the first bomb. However, Kamo once said that Koba had not taken part in the robbery. This was backed up by a police report which recorded that Koba had 'observed the ruthless bloodshed, smoking a cigarette, from the courtyard of a mansion'. According to informed sources he was at the railway station that morning, so if things went wrong he would have been able to jump on a train and flee.

As it was, the heist went off smoothly and Koba returned to the apartment he shared with Kato and their three-month-old son Yakov. Kato and the baby had been on the balcony with her family when the bombs went off, so they had witnessed the whole thing. Koba kept 15,000 roubles for himself and then he took off with his wife and child to Baku. The other gangsters took their cut and the remainder was sewn inside a mattress and sent to Lenin, who fled to Geneva. Lenin was delighted. Koba had now shown that he was not just a ruthless politician but a man of action – 'exactly the kind of person I need,' said Lenin.

When the conspirators fell out over the money, the Mensheviks expelled Koba from the Party. But they could not prove that Lenin had been involved. It was a sensitive issue. As late as 1918, Stalin launched an extraordinary libel suit to suppress the story. Any references to his career as a bank robber and an assassin were removed from the memoirs of those who had known him at the time.

Once in Baku, Stalin went to work for Rothschild again. He also met up with his old Bolshevik comrade, Sergei Alliluyev. When Alliluyev's pretty young daughter Nadya fell into the sea, Koba immediately jumped in to rescue her. She would later become his bride. It is thought that Koba also had an affair with Alliluyev's highly sexed wife Olga.

Stalin was very much at home in Baku – he called his time there his 'second baptism of fire'. The city suited his temperament. There were said to be only ten honest men in the whole of Baku: a Swede (Mr Nobel of the Nobel Brothers' Oil Company), an Armenian and eight Tartars. It was a place in which you could have someone killed for as little as three roubles – less than £12 or $20.

In August 1907 Koba visited Stuttgart, where he compared the Germans to sheep who obeyed the rules and were happy to follow wherever the ram led. Returning to Baku, he led a strike after an Azeri was murdered by Russian nationalists. He used this as an opportunity to oust the Mensheviks. Baku then became another Bolshevik stronghold.

Constant Fear

Meanwhile, he neglected Kato and their child, though no one doubted that he loved them. His wife lived in constant fear that he would be arrested and she prayed that he would give up his revolutionary ways and settle down. But Baku was hot and polluted and she grew ill so he returned her to her family in Tiflis. The next time he visited her he found her on her deathbed. She was just 22 years old.

Koba was so grief-stricken that his friends feared he might kill himself, so they took away his gun. The funeral was held in the church where they had married. Standing beside the open coffin, against character he told a friend that Kato had 'softened my heart of stone'.

'She died and with her died my last warm feelings for humanity,' he said.

Millions would suffer as a consequence. At the burial, he threw himself bodily into the grave with the coffin and he had to be pulled out by fellow mourners.

Then he noticed that some Okhranka agents had secretly joined the mourners, so he jumped over the back fence of the graveyard to make good his escape.

Comrade Koba now signed himself K. Kato – or Koba Kato. He told his comrades that his personal life was now over and that he would dedicate himself single-mindedly to socialism. Their son Yakov would be brought up in Tiflis by his in-laws, who blamed Koba for Kato's death. Koba then returned to Baku and did not see his son again for five years.

The Outfit was reconstructed in Baku, where Koba recruited a new group of terrorists and hitmen. There he agitated among the Muslim workers, who hid him in their mosques when he was on the run. In return he went into Persia with his gunmen, who made an attempt on the life of the then shah, Mohammed Ali.

In 1908, Koba visited Lenin and Plekhanov in Switzerland. He disapproved of Plekhanov because his daughter wore the latest fashions and high heels, rather than the ascetic garb of the would-be proletarian. Lenin complained, once again, that he was short of money, though his everyday needs were taken care of by his family estates in Russia.

Kidnapping and Extortion

Getting money was something Koba's gangsters could do something about, though, armed as they were from a raid on a naval arsenal, in which several guards had been murdered. First of all they seized a ship named *Nicholas I*, which was transporting four million roubles to Turkmenistan and then they turned to easier targets. Koba counterfeited money, ran protection rackets and kidnapped the children of rich families so that he could extort money from their parents. Ransoms were demanded in the name of the 'revolutionary committee'. And he could always raise money from the oil barons, who paid him to settle strikes. Not content with that, he took things a little further by having forms printed, that read: 'The Bolshevik Committee proposes that your company should pay roubles.' The money was then collected by a man carrying a pistol. In response, one of the oil barons, a Chechen named Murtuza Mukhtarov, sent some men to kill Koba. He escaped with a very bad beating, but later on he would take his revenge on all Chechens.

Koba then became more circumspect. He disguised himself as a tramp, when he would disappear for days on end, and he would either turn up extremely early or very late at meetings. He also gained a reputation as a heartless man, though he never lacked female companionship. And there were parties. After each successful heist, some of the proceeds were spent on hiring a private room in a posh restaurant, where there would be good food, singing and girls. His seduction of 18-year-old 'Comrade Plus' – Alvasi Talakvadze – brimmed over with ideological ardour, including 'discussions of social-political subjects' and 'developing class consciousness'. Once she was dispatched to take some secret documents to the

Balakhana oilfield in a child's coffin. She was told to play the role of a grieving sister who had to bury her baby brother with her bare hands – but she must be careful not to bury the coffin too deeply, so that it could be easily unearthed by his local contact later. Meanwhile Koba was having an affair with a leading female activist, the 'buxom but pretty' Ludmilla Stal, who was six years his senior.

But the authorities were moving in. While Koba was planning the robbery of the State Bank and a gold ship, there was a raid on the Party meeting. Several Cossacks were killed during the ensuing shoot-out, but Koba and the other Party leaders escaped. However, after several more raids, he was arrested and placed in Baku's Bailov Prison. The other prisoners were apprehensive. They feared Koba more than they feared the police because he was known for his witch hunts against traitors that often ended in the suspect's death. In accordance with his usual practice, Koba ordered the hits but did not wield the knife himself. He preferred to mix with criminals rather than politicians when he was behind bars and he used them as his bodyguards.

He studied Esperanto, considering it the language of the future, and he slyly put a leading Menshevik in charge of food, so that he then had to share the hampers he received from his wife. Such was his reputation as a hard man that Koba was excused domestic duties such as washing dishes and emptying the slop buckets – minions could do that. He was also reputed to be the only prisoner who could sleep soundly when condemned men were hanged in the courtyard outside his cell. And he played a cruel game called 'Madness', in which prisoners bet on how long it would take for them to drive a young prisoner insane. Koba himself was the beneficiary of acts of kindness. Finding it hard to breathe in an overcrowded cell, he had fellow terrorist Budu 'the Barrel' Mdivani lift him up to a high window.

Koba also protested against the conditions in the jail, which brought the wrath of the government soldiers down on the political prisoners – but it was said that he suffered the rifle butt blows unbowed. However, his mother Keke wept when she came to visit him. An escape plan failed so Koba was sentenced to two years' exile in Vologda. On the way, he was held in Moscow's Butyrki Prison, where many of his victims would perish when he became Stalin.

Mistresses in Exile

Always ready for female companionship, Koba took two mistresses from among the exiles in the village of Solvychegodsk when he arrived there. He was happy to cuckold his comrades if necessary. His lovers found him sensitive about his pockmarked face, his injured arm and his webbed toes but emotionally detached. He preferred malleable teenagers and uneducated peasant women who would do what they were told. In any case, they had to take second place to his revolutionary mission and he rarely kept in touch after the affair was over.

However, his affair with 23-year-old teacher Stefania Petrovskaya surprised everyone. After her sentence was over she stayed on in Solvychegodsk and then she followed him back to the Caucasus.

According to the local policeman in Solvychegodsk, Koba was 'cruel, outspoken and disrespectful' and he was fined and locked up on more than one occasion. And his habit of seeking out traitors and having them killed had not left him, even in exile. Otherwise he spent his time reading. Determined to escape, but without the necessary money, he organized a fake gambling tournament and walked off with the entire kitty of 70 roubles. Then he shaved off his beard, donned women's clothing and quickly made off.

Once back in St Petersburg he met up again with Sergei Alliluyev. He found a safe house in the porters' lodge of the Horse Guards barracks, next door to the Taurida Palace, home of the Duma, but he did not stay long. By July 1909 he had returned to Baku, where he used the codename 'the Milkman' because he operated out of a local milk bar. The Okhranka reported his presence, but did nothing about it for months. Their silence once again led to the rumour that he was an agent of the tsarist secret police.

Arrests made under the Stolypin repressions, which had begun in 1906, had weakened the Party so Koba proposed a reconciliation with the Mensheviks, which the émigré Lenin opposed. But by then Koba was seen as the leader of the Russian Bolsheviks and he wanted to concentrate more power into his own hands. He expected his comrades to be as dedicated as himself and he grew angry when they put their wives and families before their duty to the Party. When he visited Tiflis again, he organized new extortion and protection rackets, but he did not know that his father had died while he was there and had been buried in a pauper's grave.

Back in Baku, Koba changed his name again. When Stefania Petrovskaya turned up, he dropped the name 'K. Kato' and began styling himself 'K. Stefin'. But living with a woman did not soften his heart and he was soon weeding out those he considered to be traitors. The innocent perished with the guilty. At least two genuine spies survived, but the purge weakened the Party so much that members began to suspect that Koba was an Okhranka agent, out to destroy the Party from inside. Indeed it was alleged that he got rid of comrades who disagreed with him by giving their names to the Gendarmes. These assertions were supported by the experience of a leading Menshevik, who said that the Gendarmes burst in and arrested him and his judges when he was being tried for an infraction of the Party rules.

On 23 March 1910, the Milkman and his concubine Stefania were arrested. At first Koba denied any relationship with Stefania, but when she admitted cohabiting with him he asked for permission to marry her and then began calling her his wife. After she was released he broke the Party rules by writing to the governor of Baku, begging for a light sentence. The ploy worked. He was merely required to complete his term of exile in Solvychegodsk, though he was barred from the Caucasus for five years. He was also given permission to marry Stefania in the prison church, but he was transferred on the day of the ceremony. He never saw her again.

Back in Solvychegodsk, he began an affair with 22-year-old Serafima Khoroshenina. Tales of other revolutionaries' sexual adventures in exile always amused Stalin. He continued politicking through all of this, supporting Lenin against Trotsky even though he expressed disdain for those living in safety abroad. And he battled against those members who wanted the Party to become legal, like the other parties that sat in the Duma. The last thing he wanted, he said, was to turn into a 'normal person'. Lenin dismissed him as 'immature'.

Koba escaped again, but he was forced to return to Solvychegodsk. He claimed that the 70 roubles sent for his escape had been stolen by a student named Ivanian. Although Ivanian protested his innocence, Stalin waited until 1937 and then had him shot. By this time Serafima and Koba were officially cohabiting, but she was still sent to Nikolsk. Her place in his bed was immediately taken by Koba's landlady, Maria Kuzakova. Meanwhile Koba taunted the local police chief who was afraid of him, while the local priest let him use his library.

Abandoned

In 1911, when his term was up, Koba left Maria pregnant without even saying goodbye. Ordered to stay in Vologda for two months, he began a relationship with a 16-year-old schoolgirl named Pelageya Onufrieva, who was the lover of Peter Chizhikov, a comrade. She was the well-dressed daughter of a local smallholder, whom the Okhranka dubbed 'Glamourpuss'. Koba called her 'Polya' and she called him Josef or 'Oddball Osip' – Osip being the diminutive of Josef. He was close enough to her to open up and talk about Kato but then he suddenly left, telling her that he was going to St Petersburg to marry another woman. They never met again, though he did write.

Koba was arrested once again in St Petersburg. He was carrying Chizhikov's passport so he was sentenced to five years in Siberia. This was later reduced to three years. Koba volunteered to travel at his own expense back to Vologda which, though distant, was still in European Russia. There he began an affair with his landlord's daughter, but they argued about his womanizing. For instance, he flirted with the family's 16-year-old maid. He met up again with Chizhikov, but he did not renew his relationship with Polya, who had gone back to school in Totma. However, he did send her an erotic postcard.

At a Party conference in Prague, two of Koba's allies – the Armenian Suren Spandarian and the nobleman Grigoriy 'Sergo' Ordzhonikidze – were elected to the Bolshevik Central Committee. Lenin and his principal collaborator Grigory Zinoviev wanted Koba himself co-opted on to the committee but Koba soon left Vologda again. Before he did so he received a letter from Polya. He replied with a postcard, which showed a couple passionately kissing.

GRIGORY YEVSEYEVICH ZINOVIEV (1883–1936)

Born Yevsei-Gershon Aronovich Radomyslsky to lower middle-class Jewish parents, Zinoviev attended law lectures at Bern University. In 1901, he joined the Russian Social-Democratic Workers' Party and Lenin's radical *Iska* faction. Two years later he sided with the Bolsheviks and during the 1905 Revolution he was an agitator among the workers in St Petersburg.

In 1907, he became a member of the Party's Central Committee. Arrested in 1908, he was released due to ill health. He lived in exile after 1909, becoming Lenin's principal collaborator, and he accompanied Lenin when he returned to Russia in 1917. Even so, he joined Lev Kamenev in opposing the Bolshevik coup that November. After demanding that members of other socialist parties be included in the government, he resigned from the Bolshevik Central Committee. In 1919, he became chairman of the Comintern and he joined the Politburo in 1921.

A letter bearing his name was published by the British press in 1924. He was apparently ordering British Communists to conduct subversive activities. The publication of the so-called 'Zinoviev letter' was thought to have caused the downfall of Britain's first Labour government later that year.

After forming a ruling triumvirate with Stalin and Kamenev, Zinoviev helped oust Trotsky. Stalin then turned against his former allies and Zinoviev was forced out of the Politburo and expelled from the Party. In 1934 he was tried alongside Kamenev for the murder of Sergey Kirov, the Party leader in Leningrad, when he was sentenced to ten years' imprisonment. Two years later he faced a further trial, after which he was executed. However, the Soviet Supreme Court absolved him in 1988.

Back in St Petersburg in 1912, Koba's first task was to turn the Bolshevik weekly *Zvezda* (Star) into the daily *Pravda* (Truth), which was to be funded by the son of a Kazan tycoon who channelled the money through Vyacheslav Mikhaylovich Skryabin – better known under his revolutionary sobriquet 'Molotov' (from *molot*, which means hammer). Using the alias 'Vasily', Koba stayed with Tatiana Alexandrovna Slavinskaya, the wife of a revolutionary, and they began an affair. He also stayed at the Alliluyevs.

Later in 1912, Koba paid a rare visit to his son Yakov in Tiflis. Local Party members were warned that Koba was a dangerous man who was motivated by revenge. As if to prove the point, Koba ordered the murder of a sailor he had accused of being an Okhranka spy.

That year – after having been Koba Kato, Koba Stefin, Koba Safin and Koba Soli – he began calling himself Koba Stalin. The surname means 'Man of Steel' in Russian, though he still kept the Georgian forename. It was apt. In Moscow, the 9-year-old son of a Bolshevik was chatting perfectly amiably to Stalin when he

suddenly slapped the boy.

'Don't cry little boy,' he said. 'Remember today, Stalin talked to you.'

This was a Georgian custom that was rooted in local folklore. One day, it was said, a prince visited a certain Georgian village. When he had gone, a peasant slapped his son and said: 'Remember today, a prince visited our house.'

Stalin was arrested on his return to St Petersburg. He had been betrayed by Roman Malinovsky, who was praised as a genuine proletarian talent by Lenin, but who was, in fact, an Okhranka agent. Stalin was sentenced to yet another period of

Zinoviev was part of the Bolshevik Central Committee in exile. With Lenin and Kamenev, he stoked the fires of Marxism beyond the reach of tsarist police

YAKOV IOSIFOVICH DZHUGASHVILI
AKA YAKOV STALIN (1907–1943)

Yakov was Stalin's son with his first wife Kato, but he never got on with his father. Things got worse when he moved to Moscow and married a priest's daughter. When Stalin disapproved, Yakov tried to shoot himself, but he failed. While his stepmother Nadya tended his wounds, Stalin disparaged the boy, saying, 'The fool – he can't even shoot straight.'

As an artillery officer in the Red Army,

Yakov was captured when the Germans invaded. The Germans offered to trade him for Field Marshal Friedrich Paulus, who was captured at the Battle of Stalingrad, but Stalin turned the offer down, saying, 'I will not trade a marshal for a lieutenant.' Hitler also suggested swapping Yakov for his nephew Leo Raubal, but Stalin rejected this offer too. Yakov died in captivity after being shot while trying to escape in 1943.

Stalin was arrested in 1913 and sent into exile in Turukhansk in Siberia; he lived in the village of Kostino and was then transferred to Kureika on the edge of the Arctic Circle where he remained until called up for the army in 1916

exile, this time for three years. At Narym, far beyond the Urals, he again avoided his share of domestic chores and introduced himself by his real name Dzhugashvili. On this occasion he attracted the attentions of a young housewife named Lukeria Tihomirova. After only a month he escaped again and resumed his criminal career.

On 24 September 1912 the Outfit ambushed a mail coach carrying a huge sum of money in Tiflis. They escaped empty-handed after an exchange of gunfire that killed at least three policemen and left around nine other people dead or injured. Eighteen gunmen were arrested while Stalin fled back to St Petersburg. Still on the run, he managed to edit *Pravda*, oversee the Bolshevik nominations for the elections to the Duma and write the election manifesto. His selection of candidates was not a great success, however – of the six Bolsheviks elected to the Duma two were Okhranka agents. Six Mensheviks were also elected and Stalin again urged a reconciliation which Lenin once more opposed.

Furnished with false passports, Stalin travelled to meet Lenin in Cracow – he had his latest lover Valentina Lobova, wife of an Okhranka agent, in tow. That December, Lenin invited Stalin to return. This time Lenin's wife Krupskaya addressed the invitation to 'K. St.'. Again he travelled with Valentina. Cracow was in Galicia, which was then part of the Austro-Hungarian Empire. The rest of Poland was occupied by Prussia and Russia. On his way to Cracow, Stalin stopped to eat in a station restaurant. After addressing the Polish waiter in Russian he found he could get no service, so he flung his plate furiously on the floor and stormed out. He could not understand that for the Poles Russian was the language of the oppressor.

Instead of returning to St Petersburg, Lenin asked Stalin to stay in Cracow and write an essay on the future of non-Russian nationalities within the empire – a subject on which he was considered to be an expert. In the essay, Stalin outlined the blueprint of the Soviet Union, in which the separate nations would appear to be autonomous while they were in fact under the control of a central authority. *Marxism and the National Question*, written 1912–13, was the first of Stalin's published pieces to carry the by-line K. St. It was highly praised by Lenin. As this was the article that made the 33-year-old Georgian's reputation, he kept the sobriquet Stalin. It had echoes of Lenin and some of it was perhaps borrowed from his former lover Ludmilla Stal, who worked closely with him in exile.

Betrayed Again

While he was in Cracow, Stalin became friends with Malinovsky, who had betrayed him in St Petersburg. Malinovsky was a convicted burglar and rapist who was enjoying the handsome Okhranka salary of 8,000 roubles a year – 1,000 roubles more than the director of the Imperial Police. He was also a man after Stalin's own heart, someone who was fervent about the cause, so they spent much of their time denouncing treacherous Bolsheviks to each other. Meanwhile, Stalin caved in to Lenin's view that there should be no reconciliation with the Mensheviks.

Stalin then moved on to Vienna, where he stayed in the Schönbrunnerschloss Strasse apartment of a young nobleman called Alexander Troyanovsky. It overlooked the route that Emperor Franz Josef took every day between his residence in the Schönbrunn Palace and his office at the Hofburg. The Troyanovsky's nanny would later complain of the difficulty of washing Stalin's shirts and underwear. Also in Vienna at the time were Josip Broz – who later took the pseudonym Tito – and 23-year-old Adolf Hitler, who was living in a men's dosshouse in Brigettenau, a world away from the posh apartment in which Stalin was living. While he was in Vienna, Stalin met Nikolay Ivanovich Bukharin, who would later help him to power, and Trotsky, whom Stalin already disliked. The feeling was mutual because Trotsky hated Stalin on sight.

When Stalin returned to St Petersburg, an article was published denouncing Malinovsky as an Okhranka agent. Stalin – then also known as Ioska Koriavyi (Joe Pox) – used bully-boy tactics in an attempt to crush the rumour. Meanwhile Malinovsky was betraying each member of the Central Committee in turn to the Okhranka. When it was Stalin's turn, Malinovsky invited him to a Bolshevik fundraiser. Stalin said he was not in the mood, but Malinovsky was insistent, even lending Stalin a shirt and tie for the occasion. The event was raided and once again Stalin tried to escape in women's clothing, but this time he was seized by the Okhranka. He was sentenced to four years in Turukhansk, northern Siberia, even though he protested that he was not Dzhugashvili, the man they were after. From Turukhansk there would be no escape. Thanks to Malinovsky, the Okhranka thwarted every effort to free Comrade Stalin.

Again Stalin used his time in exile to read voraciously. He stole books from the communal library, refusing to share them with other exiles. They protested so vehemently that Stalin had to be moved, perhaps taking his newly acquired books with him. He ended up on the edge of the Arctic Circle. As winter drew in and the temperature headed for minus 60 degrees Celsius, he wrote to Tatiana Slavinskaya, begging for help. She sent warm clothes and others sent money. But money promised by Malinovsky was diverted by the Jewish Bolshevik leader Yakov Sverdlov and funds promised by Zinoviev did not arrive. Eventually Malinovsky was exposed as a traitor and he was shot after the Revolution. Meanwhile Stalin and Sverdlov fell out over the money, with Sverdlov condemning Stalin as an 'individualist' – a gross insult to a Bolshevik, who is supposed to surrender to the collective. The two men stopped talking.

Sverdlov particularly disapproved of Stalin when the 34-year-old philanderer got 13-year-old orphan Lidia Pereprygin drunk and then seduced her. Stalin then moved into the two-roomed log cabin that she shared with her sister and five brothers. The lovers lived in a filthy room that could only be reached through the cowshed. Her brothers disliked their unwanted house guest, particularly when Lidia fell pregnant. When Stalin's Gendarme guard caught the couple *in flagrante delicto* Stalin promised

FIRST WORLD WAR

On 28 June 1914 a group of Serbian nationalists sought to liberate the southern Slavs of the Austro-Hungarian Empire by assassinating Archduke Franz Ferdinand, heir presumptive to the Austrian throne, in Sarajevo. In retaliation, Austria declared war on Serbia. Tsarist Russia came to Serbia's defence because of the Slavic ties between the two countries. After the German Kaiser had urged Austria-Hungary to attack, he warned Russia not to mobilize and insisted that the French should stay neutral, but both Russia and France ignored these demands. Germany then declared war on France and began attacking through Belgium, whose neutrality was guaranteed by Great Britain. Italy and Japan sided with Russia and the Western Allies, while Turkey and its Ottoman Empire joined the Central Powers.

The development of the machine gun by the Allies halted the Germany's western advance. There was then a prolonged period of stalemate as the German and Allied armies faced each other in lines of trenches and barbed wire across northern France, from the Channel to the Swiss border. Periodic battles resulted in massive slaughter, but few gains. The British sought to blockade Germany at sea, while the Germans used submarines in an attempt to cut Britain's Atlantic supply lines. There was more fighting in the Dardanelles, the Middle East, Germany's African colonies and along the Italian front.

In the east, the battle was more fluid. The Germans' superior tactics and greater industrial output brought them battlefield victories, but the Russians could call on massive manpower. However, they also had to defend the Caucasus against the Turks. Tsar Nicholas II took command of the Russian forces that faced the Germans in September 1915. An offensive was launched in 1916 which had its successes, but cost the Russians a million men. This senseless slaughter sounded the death knell for the Russian monarchy.

Although the tsar was deposed by the February Revolution in 1917, Russia continued fighting. However, the Germans realized that there was a good chance that Russia would withdraw from the war if they gave Lenin and the other anti-war socialists safe passage through German territory. They could then concentrate their efforts against the Western Allies. By the time the Brest-Litovsk Treaty between Russia and Germany was signed on 3 March 1918, the United States had entered the war on the side of the Allies. At the same time, Britain had developed the tank, which broke the stalemate and proved a war-winning weapon. The resulting blockade brought Germany to its knees. The fighting in the west ended with an Armistice on 11 November 1918 and a peace treaty was signed in Versailles in the following year.

In 1914, Cossack brigades fought the Germans and Austro-Hungarians on the Eastern Front, and the Turks to the south. From the late 18th century, they had served the tsars as soldiers and police, and were thus widely loathed

him that he would marry Lidia when she came of age. Stalin then used his influence to get the Gendarme transferred and he used his replacement as his valet.

Europe at War

As Europe was plunged into the First World War, Stalin found little to complain about except that he had nothing in English to read and he was left to discuss international politics with his dog. That winter, Stalin grew close to the local Tungus and Ostyak tribesmen who called him Osip or 'Pockmarked Oska'. As the wolves circled the village, the tribesmen taught Stalin to hunt and fish through holes in the ice on the river. They also taught him to be stoical when men were lost in the harsh conditions.

'Why should we have pity for men?' they said. 'We can always make more of them, but a horse? Try making a horse.'

He took this to heart.

In later years Stalin said that he nearly died in the snow, but it seems he exaggerated his tales about his life in Siberia, though no one dared contradict him. However, life was certainly tough for those around him. Lidia gave birth in December 1914, but the child died soon afterwards.

Like Lenin, Stalin hoped the Germans would defeat Russia, because that would hasten the Revolution and bring about a European civil war between the proletariat and the bourgeoisie. They were confident that the workers would win the struggle. However, Trotsky's brother-in-law Kamenev, the editor of *Pravda*, instructed the Bolshevik members of the Duma to oppose the war. He was arrested and exiled to

Siberia. Stalin accused him of betraying the Revolution. When the two men met up again, Kamenev gave Stalin a copy of Machiavelli's *The Prince* – though Stalin had long ago adopted Machiavelli's principle of ruling by force.

At a particularly drunken dinner, Kamenev asked the guests what their greatest pleasure was. Some answered that it was the love of women, while others unsmilingly avowed that it was dialectical materialism, which drove the engine of history towards the workers' paradise.

'My greatest pleasure is to choose one's victim,' said Stalin, 'prepare one's plans minutely, sate one's implacable vengeance, then go to bed. Nothing is sweeter in this world.'

Kamenev called this 'Stalin's Theory of Sweet Revenge' and it showed that Stalin knew himself all too well. Indeed, Stalin had already chosen his victim. He and his friend Spandarian, who was also in exile, had decided to put Kamenev on trial for betraying the Revolution. Though Stalin had the casting vote, this time he stayed his hand. Another exile was being tried at the same time, a man called Petukhov, who told of when Spandarian had robbed a shop of food and warm clothing. Sverdlov said that Spandarian should be tried for theft and Stalin insisted that both Kamenev and Spandarian should be expelled. Spandarian died of tuberculosis soon afterwards.

During his exile, Stalin received a parcel from Olga Alliluyeva. It contained a suit. In the pocket was a note from Nadya, Olga's daughter, who was now 14 years old. And Lidia was soon pregnant again. It was perhaps no coincidence that Stalin then disappeared on a long fishing trip. Not even his police guard knew where he was. It was rumoured that he had escaped, so a peasant was jailed for 18 months for lending him a boat and another person seems to have been sent to prison for aiding him. Stalin himself remained unpunished when he returned. Locals said he had been absent to avoid marrying his teenage mistress.

In October 1916, with the war raging, Stalin was conscripted. He could easily have stayed behind because his injured arm would have prevented him from passing the medical. Instead, he headed off gallantly towards the front, leaving Lidia behind. Later he discovered that she had given birth to his son Alexander. He never contacted her again, but he did not forget his time in Turukhansk. When he came to power he built a huge Gulag there. It was to have been supplied by the 'Railway of Death', the building of which cost the lives of tens of thousands of men, but the line was never completed.

The conscripts sang and drank all the way to Krasnoyarsk, where the medical officer found Stalin unfit for military service. He was to spend the last four months of his exile in Achinsk, where he was joined by Vera Shveitzer, Spandarian's former mistress. At one time he was a morose presence in Kamenev's house, where he annoyed Kamenev's wife with his pipe smoke.

CHAPTER FIVE

THE REVOLUTIONARY

With Stalin as Lenin's trusted lieutenant, the Bolsheviks seized power, ruthlessly excluding those who disagreed with them. Rivals within the Party or outside it were executed or confined to labour camps on the flimsiest of pretexts. A murderous civil war raged, but Lenin and Stalin thought that this was a fair price to pay if their political theories were to be put to the test. However, the day would come when Lenin would repudiate his protégé.

WITH TSAR NICHOLAS AWAY AT THE FRONT FROM **1915** ONWARDS, THE TSARINA ALEXANDRA HAD BEEN LEFT IN CHARGE OF THE GOVERNMENT IN ST PETERSBURG, WHICH HAD BEEN RENAMED PETROGRAD TO SOUND LESS GERMAN. But her authority was undermined by her dependence on Rasputin. Even his murder in 1916 did not help. Riots and rebellions abounded and on 26 February 1917 50 people were cut down by the Cossacks.

Shortly afterwards the police headquarters was burned down and the arsenal was seized. The Petrograd Soviet of Workers' and Soldiers' Deputies elected an Executive Committee under the chairmanship of the Menshevik Karlo Chkheidze on 27 February.

Tsarina Alexandra was unpopular in Russia because of her cold and curt German manner

The tsar tried to return to Petrograd to take control of the situation, but his train was stuck in Pskov. On 2 March 1917 he was forced to abdicate in favour of his brother, Grand Duke Michael. Kamenev proposed sending a telegram congratulating him on his decision, but Stalin disapproved. Following the tsar's abdication, a provisional government was established in the Taurida Palace under Prince Georgi Lvov, which competed for legitimacy with the Petrograd Soviet.

The exiles were now free to go so Stalin, Shveitzer and Kamenev made their way to the station to take the train to Petrograd. Along the way, Kamenev made speeches in which he challenged any local orators who did not support the Bolshevik cause. Stalin was no orator so he stayed in the background, brooding. On 12 March, they arrived in Petrograd. The city was a tumult of lawless celebration and street fighting. People had sex openly on the streets and pornographic descriptions of Rasputin's orgies were circulated. The supposed lesbian activities of the tsarina were a central feature of the pamphlets. Women wore soldiers' uniforms, while thieves and prostitutes elected their own soviets.

Stalin Takes Charge

No one was in charge – Lenin was in Switzerland and Trotsky was in New York. But Stalin was on the scene and Kamenev was on the sidelines. Aided by Molotov, Stalin took charge. He billeted himself at the Alliluyevs' apartment before going to the Bolsheviks' headquarters, which had established itself in the mansion of Nicholas

GRIGORY YEFIMOVICH RASPUTIN (1872?–1916)

Born Grigory Yefimohich Novykh in the village of Pokrovskoye, Siberia, his licentious behaviour earned him the nickname Rasputin, 'the debauched one'. He joined the Khlysty sect of flagellants and preached that the way to come close to God was through sexual exhaustion. The ritual of 'rejoicing' – that is, sexual orgies – brought him many followers.

By the time he reached St Petersburg, Rasputin [*seen above with the ladies-in-waiting*] had a powerful reputation as a mystic, a healer and a clairvoyant but his rise to royal influence began in 1905, when he was introduced at court. Tsar Nicholas's son Alexis was a haemophiliac and Rasputin's assistance was sought when all else had failed. It was found that he could successfully ease the child's condition, perhaps through hypnotism.

'God has seen your tears and heard your prayers,' Rasputin told the tsarina. 'Fear not, the child will not die.'

Rasputin also came up with some surprisingly practical advice. For instance, he halted the use of leeches, whose saliva contains an anticoagulant and he put a stop to the administration of aspirin, which prevents the blood from clotting. He also kept the boy away from doctors and he recommended rest, which allowed the natural healing processes to work.

While Rasputin was a paragon of chastity and humility at court, he continued with his scandalous ways in the outside world. In 1911, the prime minister drew up a long bill of Rasputin's offences and the tsar expelled him from court. But he was soon recalled by the tsarina, who feared for her son's life. However, when Tsar Nicholas was called to the front during the First World War, the tsarina was left in charge of the nation. Rasputin then began to meddle in government affairs. The tsarina and the mystic were so close that many thought they were lovers. Meanwhile Tsarina Alexandra became increasingly unpopular because she was German by birth.

An attempt was made on Rasputin's life on 29 June 1914 when Khionia Guseva, a former prostitute who had been one of his followers, stabbed him in the belly when he was visiting his wife and children in Pokrovskoye. 'I have killed the Antichrist,' she cried. Rasputin recovered after surgery, though he continued to take opium for pain relief.

Then on 30 December 1916, a gang of noblemen fed him poisoned cakes and wine. When he fell into a coma he was shot four times by Prince Felix Yussupov, a homosexual who had been rebuffed by Rasputin. A second assassin pulled out a knife and castrated the mystic before throwing his severed penis across the room. Rasputin was then tied up and thrown into the icy river Neva, where he finally drowned.

II's mistress, the ballerina Mathilde Kseshinskaya, opposite the Winter Palace.

On 15 March Stalin and Kamenev took charge of *Pravda*, ousting Molotov. Stalin was then appointed as a Bolshevik representative to the Executive Committee of the Soviet in the Taurida Palace. He sought a reconciliation with the Mensheviks, who were still backing the war. Lenin, on the other hand, attacked the Provisional Government and called for an immediate peace with Germany. This suited the Kaiser so on 27 March the Germans arranged for Lenin to return to Russia across German territory, in the famous 'sealed train'. When Lenin arrived in Russia on 3 April Stalin rushed to support him, dumping Kamenev in the process. Lenin shunned the official greetings when he disembarked at Finland Station in Petrograd. Instead he jumped on top of an armoured car and addressed the crowd, telling them that the Provisional Government was deceiving the people. The Bolsheviks must overthrow them and end the imperialist war, he declared, waving his bourgeois umbrella. He must have cut a curious figure in his tweed suit and Homburg hat. The hat was later replaced with a workers' cap.

Lenin and Kamenev help lay the foundation stone for a temporary monument to Marx and Engels in 1918. All of his life, Kamenev had been preparing to become a professional revolutionary and he relished his role of leading Bolshevik

LEV BORISOVICH KAMENEV (1883–1936)

Born to middle-class parents who had been part of the Russian revolutionary movement of the 1870s, Kamenev dedicated himself to becoming a professional revolutionary. He began by joining the Russian Social-Democratic Workers' Party in 1901 and the Bolshevik faction in 1903. In 1908, he emigrated to western Europe to work with Lenin, who sent him back in 1914 to lead the Bolshevik members of the Duma in their opposition to the First World War. He was arrested in November 1914 and sent to Siberia.

After the February Revolution in 1917, he returned to Petrograd to organize the Bolsheviks alongside Stalin. He advocated the support of the Provisional Government, but this move was rejected by Lenin when he returned to Russia. Together with his friend Zinoviev, Kamenev opposed the October Revolution. Nevertheless he was elected to the Politburo and he became chairman of the Central Executive Committee.

When Lenin fell ill, he formed part of a ruling triumvirate with Stalin and Zinoviev, thereby pushing Trotsky out of contention. But then Stalin turned on him and he was forced out of the Politburo and expelled from the Party. After the Leningrad Party leader Sergey Kirov was assassinated in December 1934, Kamenev and Zinoviev were tried secretly for complicity in his murder. They were then accused of conspiring to murder Stalin and were forced to appear in the first public show trial of the Great Purge. Kamenev confessed to fabricated charges in the vain hope of saving his family, but he was shot and his wife died in the Gulag. Both Kamenev and Zinoviev were cleared of all charges by the Soviet Supreme Court in 1988.

Many people thought Lenin was out of touch, a spent force. But the Provisional Government could only establish its legitimacy in an election which was months away. In the interval, Lenin believed that the Bolsheviks could seize power. First of all he went to work with Stalin at *Pravda*. The more radical Bolsheviks called for an armed insurrection, but Lenin counselled caution. Nevertheless, Stalin defended Lenin against attacks by Kamenev and in the elections for the Central Committee on 29 April he came third after Lenin and Zinoviev. The Central Committee then selected Lenin, Zinoviev, Stalin and Kamenev as its decision-making Politburo. Finally, Trotsky returned from America to become the dazzling star of the Revolution. Stalin avoided speaking at public meetings because of his comical Georgian accent.

On 3 June, Nadya Alliluyeva and her sister Anna went to see Stalin at the first congress of the Soviets. They witnessed the moment when the Menshevik Irakli Tsereteli clashed with Lenin.

'There is not a party in Russia that dares say, "Just place power in our hands,"' Menekin declared.

Lenin then jumped from his seat and yelled, 'There is such a party!'

While Lenin, Zinoviev and Kamenev made speeches, the Bolsheviks were controlled from behind the scenes by Stalin and Sverdlov. Stalin was known for his work in the Caucasus and he was in touch with the mood of the rank and file because he had stayed in Russia while those whom they considered flashy intellectuals had sought safety abroad. He became reconciled with Molotov and they moved into a large apartment with three other comrades. But while Stalin continued his relationship with Ludmilla Stal, he also stole Molotov's girlfriend Marusya from him. And he could hardly be blind to the fact that he had a fan in Nadya Alliluyeva, who turned up at the offices of *Pravda* with her sister Anna to see him.

Lenin and Stalin approved an armed demonstration by the Military Organization, the armed wing of the Bolshevik Party which now boasted a following of 60,000 soldiers, but the Mensheviks saw this as a Bolshevik conspiracy to seize power. When the Soviet voted against it, Lenin called it off. A week later, the Soviet organized its own demonstration, which the Bolsheviks hijacked. Meanwhile an offensive against the Germans was ordered by the Provisional Government's minister of war, Aleksandr Kerensky, who was also vice-chairman of the Petrograd Soviet. He was hoping to bolster the position of the Provisional Government, but the operation was a disaster.

Stamps played a big part in Soviet propaganda: here, Stalin is seen as heroic comrade-in-arms to Lenin

Under Siege

On 16 July, the failed offensive against the Germans sparked off spontaneous demonstrations in Petrograd. Workers and soldiers were demanding that power be given to the Soviet. Lenin had returned to Finland by this time but the Military Organization took matters into their own hands. The Bolshevik First Machine-Gun Regiment marched on the Taurida Palace, demanding 'All power to the Soviets' – Lenin's slogan – and other armed Bolsheviks took over the streets. Encouraged by Stalin, sailors from the Kronstadt naval base murdered their officers and landed in Petrograd – though they seemed happier strolling the boulevards with scantily clad girlfriends than joining in any revolutionary action.

Instead of seizing power, however, the Petrograd Soviet found itself under siege. Demonstrators flocked to the Kseshinskaya Mansion in the hope of finding some leadership, but Lenin's short speech failed to inspire them. Then it rained. The Soviet was now perceived as a toothless talking shop and the Bolshevik Central Committee appeared to be in retreat. At this point, the justice minister announced that Lenin had been funded by Imperial Germany, which turned the troops against him. Kerensky seized his opportunity by sending a group of loyal soldiers to the Kseshinskaya Mansion to arrest the Bolshevik leader, but Stalin managed to smuggle him out. However, Stalin then had no alternative but to give up possession of the mansion and broker a peace, surrendering other Bolshevik strongholds at the same time.

Lenin kept moving house as Kerensky's men tried to track him down. Many senior Bolsheviks thought Lenin should consider giving himself up in order to stand trial and Lenin agreed with them, but Stalin argued against it. He managed to convince Lenin that he would not be safe in the hands of the police or the military. Stalin then made it his business to smuggle the now clean-shaven Lenin out of Petrograd. First of all he hid him in a worker's shack at Razliv, 15 miles north of the city, and then he moved him on to a barn in Finland. With Lenin safely in hiding, Stalin wrote a barrage of articles condemning Kerensky's attack on the leader of the Bolshevik party, calling it the 'new Dreyfus Affair'. He wrote so much that he got calluses on his fingers.

Fearing arrest, Stalin moved into the Alliluyevs' new apartment in the suburbs.

ALEKSANDR FYODOROVICH KERENSKY (1881–1970)

While studying law at St Petersburg University, Kerensky was attracted to the *Narodniki* – or Populist – movement. He joined the Socialist Revolutionary Party after graduating in 1904 and in 1912 he was elected to the Duma. Unlike other Socialists, he supported the Russian war effort during the First World War, but he became increasingly disillusioned by the tsar's leadership failures so in 1917 he urged the dissolution of the monarchy. He became minister of justice in the Duma's Provisional Government and deputy chairman of the Petrograd Soviet of Workers' and Soldiers' Deputies, the only person to hold a position in both governing bodies.

In May 1917 he became minister of war and he toured the front in an effort to raise morale. However, his June offensive proved to be a disaster, though a reorganization of the Provisional Government made him prime minister. Although he retained the popular vote he alienated politicians to the left and right and he eventually assumed dictatorial powers. He was away at the front when the Bolsheviks took over and was unable to raise enough loyalist troops to regain power. In 1918 he went into exile in western Europe, moving to the United States in 1940.

On one occasion he fell asleep with his pipe in his mouth, almost burning the place down. Olga made him a military-style tunic in imitation of the one Kerensky favoured, which Stalin wore with a flat cap like Lenin's. Nadya idolized Stalin and they grew closer. Olga disapproved of the affair between 37-year-old Stalin and her 15-year-old daughter, partly because Olga and Stalin had themselves been lovers. It was even rumoured that Stalin was Nadya's father. But Olga could not stop the relationship and the two were soon seen as a couple.

At the sixth Party congress in July, Stalin demanded a separate revolution in Russia, rather than wait around for the whole of Europe to be engulfed by rebellion, as Marx had predicted. Stalin's call was supported by continuing social unrest,

Kerensky toured the front in 1917 in an effort to raise morale, but his June offensive turned out to be a disaster

THE DREYFUS AFFAIR

In 1894 Captain Alfred Dreyfus, a French army officer of Jewish origin, was accused of selling military secrets to the Germans. He was tried and convicted and given a life sentence on Devil's Island off the coast of South America. It then became clear that the real culprit was Major Marie-Charles-Ferdinand Esterhazy, but the army refused to reopen the case.

France was split between those who believed that Dreyfus had only been convicted because he was a Jew and those who believed that justice had been done. It was then discovered that the principal evidence against Dreyfus was forged, at which point Esterhazy fled to England. Dreyfus was retried in 1899 but he was again found guilty, though with extenuating circumstances. In 1906 he was cleared by a civilian court and his military rank was restored.

which provoked Kerensky to appoint the Siberian Cossack general, Lavr Kornilov, as commander-in-chief of the Russian army. Kerensky directed Kornilov to restore order by sending troops into Petrograd, but Kornilov responded by threatening to launch a military coup. Alarmed, Kerensky dismissed him and became commander-in-chief himself. Undeterred, Kornilov decided to proceed with his advance on Petrograd. Kerensky found he had no troops to call on at that point so he had to appeal to the Petrograd Soviet for help in defending the city. The alliance was successful and Kornilov was arrested, after which Kerensky appointed a five-man directorate, with himself as a director. But Kerensky was now dependent on cocaine and morphine and he had lost any real authority. On the other hand, the incident had greatly increased the standing of the Bolsheviks, who were in the ascendancy with the factories and the military.

Kamenev, Zinoviev and Trotsky emerged from hiding and Trotsky once again stepped into the limelight, overshadowing Stalin on the Central Executive Committee and at *Pravda*. Kamenev tried to negotiate a coalition with the Mensheviks, but Lenin now controlled the Moscow and Petrograd Soviets. From Helsinki, he issued his historic proclamation to the Bolsheviks.

'History will not forgive us if we do not assume power now.'

Stalin and Trotsky backed Lenin, but they were outvoted on the Central Committee.

October Revolution

In October 1917, a clean-shaven Lenin wearing an ill-fitting curly wig arrived on Stalin's doorstep. At a secret meeting, he managed to convince the Central Committee that the time for an armed uprising had come. Only Kamenev and Zinoviev were against the idea, fearing that it was too risky. Although no plan had been drawn up, Stalin urged the Committee to pick a date for the insurrection. It had to be soon because the Germans were advancing towards Petrograd.

Trotsky headed the Soviet Military–Revolutionary Committee, which prepared for the Revolution. On 21 October (Old Style), the Military–Revolutionary Committee assumed command of the Petrograd Garrison and then took over the famous Peter and Paul Fortress in the centre of the city. At dawn on 24 October Kerensky sent troops in to smash the presses of Stalin's newspapers and in response Stalin called in the Red Guards, including a company from the Volkynia regiment. On that day he managed to circulate the papers that were already printed and get the presses running again, but he missed the crucial

The man who arrived on Stalin's doorstep: Lenin in disguise, clean-shaven, bewigged and ready for power

Central Committee meeting at which assignments for the coup were handed out. This allowed Trotsky to allege that Stalin had 'missed the Revolution'. But Trotsky was not at the meeting either. Neither was Lenin, who was still in hiding.

That evening, Lenin visited Stalin. With his wig glued in place and bandages swaddled around his face, Lenin then took a tram to the Smolny Institute, which now housed the Bolsheviks' headquarters. He was stopped by a government patrol, but they instantly dismissed him as a harmless drunk. The Red Guards refused him entry to the Institute because he had no papers, but the crowd pushed

The storming of the Winter Palace: this key incident in the Russian Revolution took place under somewhat farcical circumstances, but it was later re-enacted and put on celluloid to much more heroic effect

them aside. Safely inside, Lenin doffed his cap and his wig came off with it.

Stalin arrived in the early hours of 25 October, when an emergency meeting of the Central Committee was called. While the Bolshevik-dominated Military–Revolutionary Committee put the coup into action, Lenin began drafting decrees. He was still in his comical disguise. Gunfire could be heard, though there was no actual fighting. In quick succession, the power station, the main post office, the train stations, most of the bridges, the State Bank and the telephone exchange fell to the revolutionaries. Kerensky realized that the only way he could reverse the situation was to get troops from the front, so he left the Winter Palace and drove out of the city.

A Congress of the Soviets had been called. While the meeting was taking place, the Bolsheviks began to surround the Winter Palace, which was still technically the seat of government. Meanwhile Lenin, Stalin, Trotsky, Molotov and Abel Yenukidze, a revolutionary Stalin had known from the seminary, began discussing the structure of the new government. Lenin did not want to have 'ministers' as such, so Trotsky suggested that they should be called 'People's Commissars'. The government itself would be the 'Council of People's Commissars' and its chairman would be prime minister, in effect.

Lenin proposed that Trotsky should be chairman, but Trotsky refused on the grounds that no Jew could be premier of Russia. Instead, he insisted that Lenin should take the post. Lenin then suggested that Stalin should be People's Commissar of the Nationalities. After that, Lenin made his first appearance before the Soviet, having been introduced by Trotsky. He then claimed power. The Mensheviks objected, calling Lenin's actions 'criminal and insane'. They walked out, boycotting the Congress and writing themselves out of history.

While the Bolsheviks manoeuvred for power at the Smolny Institute, Kerensky's cabinet still held out in the Winter Palace, which was defended by several squadrons of Cossacks, 400 military cadets and a Women's Shock Battalion. Lenin knew it had to be taken at all costs and he threatened to have the Bolshevik leaders shot if they did not storm it. Trotsky and the Military–Revolutionary Committee ordered the Peter and Paul Fortress across the Neva to fire on the palace but the six-inch guns there had not been cleaned, so three-inch training guns were trundled into position – but no one could find any three-inch shells.

At 6 pm, the military cadets at the palace left to find some food, because they had not eaten all day. They were quickly followed by the Cossacks and some of the Women's Shock Battalion. The agreed signal for the storming of the Winter Palace was a red lantern on top of the Peter and Paul Fortress flagpole, but no one could find one, so a commissar went in search of a suitable light. It was the wrong colour and he fell in a bog.

Meanwhile, the Bolsheviks ordered the cruisers *Aurora* and *Amur* to steam upriver to bombard the palace. They issued an ultimatum, but when it expired nothing happened.

The steely gaze of Lenin in his Kremlin office in 1918 as he seeks to transform Russia into a socialist utopia. Uppermost in his mind was his own dictum: 'No revolution is worth anything unless it can defend itself'

The mayor of Petrograd pledged to defend the Provisional Government. Armed with an umbrella he marched on the palace followed by the councillors, who were carrying salami as provisions for the troops. They were joined by Molotov singing 'La Marseillaise'. At a Red Guard checkpoint, the commander pledged not to fire on unarmed Russians. In that case, the mayor asked what action the Red Guard would take if they went ahead. The commander replied, 'We will spank you.'

Finally, the *Aurora* fired a blank shell, sending the Women's Shock Battalion into shock. The gunners of the Peter and Paul Fortress had cleaned their guns by then. They fired 36 six-inch shells, only two of which hit the palace. As armoured cars raked the walls with machine-gun fire, small groups of soldiers and sailors discovered that not only was the palace undefended – the doors were not even locked. At 2 am they entered in force. In the tsar's dining room Kerensky's ministers were still debating who should be their new director, but they gave in and decided to surrender just as the door opened. The Provisional Government was arrested and the Red Guards began looting the tsar's wine cellar. Some of the Women's Shock Battalion were raped. Three years later the storming of the Winter Palace was re-enacted and filmed to much more heroic effect.

Once the Winter Palace was in Bolshevik hands, Lenin took off his wig and wiped off his make-up. He was now the leader of Russia but he was exhausted, so he went to sleep on a pile of newspapers with Trotsky. Stalin continued drafting an appeal to the people until he too fell asleep.

The Congress of Soviets met at 1 pm but Lenin did not appear until 8.40 pm, when he called for the construction of a socialist order. At 2.30 am on the next morning the members of the new government were announced and Stalin was among them. He moved into the Smolny Institute where the new government had gathered to begin building the new Russia. Trotsky and Kamenev proposed abolishing capital punishment in the army.

'What nonsense,' yelled Lenin at once. 'How can you have a revolution without firing squads?'

FELIKS EDMUNDOVICH DZERZHINSKY (1877–1926)

A Polish nobleman turned revolutionary, Dzerzhinsky joined the Lithuanian Social Democratic Party in 1895. Although the Russian Imperial Police arrested him five times between 1897 and 1908, he managed to escape from exile on each occasion. He took part in the Russian Revolution of 1905 and in the years that followed he persuaded his colleagues to unite with the Russian Social-Democratic Workers' Party.

Arrested again in 1912, he remained in captivity until the Revolution of February 1917. In the following July he joined the Bolshevik Central Committee, where he played a prominent part in the October Revolution, and in December he became head of the newly formed Cheka. In this role he helped to stabilize Lenin's regime by arbitrarily eliminating anyone he considered to be a political opponent of the Soviet state. A ruthless, fanatical Communist, he organized Russia's first concentration camps.

During the Russo-Polish War of 1919–20 Dzerzhinsky joined the committee that would have been Poland's Bolshevik government had Russia won the war. After the end of the Russian Civil War, the Cheka was changed into the GPU or *Gosudarstvennoye Politicheskoye Upravlenie* (State Political Directorate). It later became the OGPU or *Ob'edinennoe Gosudarstvennoe Politicheskoe Upravlenie* (Unified State Political Directorate) which oversaw the 'corrective' labour camps. This did not diminish Dzerzhinsky's power. He had a staff of 250,000 and was responsible for the execution of 140,000 people. From 1921 to 1924, he was also minister of the interior with an office in the notorious Lubyanka, the secret police headquarters and prison. A staunch supporter of Stalin, he died after a two-hour long speech to the Bolshevik Central Committee, when he violently denounced Trotsky, Kamenev and Zinoviev. On hearing of his death Stalin eulogized Dzerzhinsky as '... a devout knight of the proletariat'.

There were more pressing problems. The Menshevik-led railway workers went on strike and Kerensky rallied the Cossacks outside Petrograd, while Stalin organized the defence of the city. Stalin, Trotsky and Lenin quickly formed themselves into the all-powerful inner core of the administration. They began negotiating peace with Germany and then established a government in the form of the Council of People's Commissars. Lenin then created the All-Russian Extraordinary Commission for Combating Counter-revolution and Sabotage (Cheka) – his own all-powerful secret police force. Some people asked him why, in that case, the government needed the People's Commissariat for Justice. Wouldn't it be better to have an honestly named Commissariat of Annihilation?

'That's exactly how it is going to be,' Lenin replied. 'We are engaged in annihilation.'

He insisted that everything would be smashed to pieces and he demanded more hangings and shootings.

'If we can't shoot White Guard saboteurs, what kind of revolution is this?' he said. 'Nothing but talk and a bowl of mush.' And he berated his comrades for not being tough enough.

But Trotsky and Stalin were extremely tough.

'We must put an end once and for all to the Papist–Quaker babble about the sanctity of human life,' Trotsky said. And when he heard that the Estonian Bolsheviks were proposing to round up traitors and liquidate them, he said: 'The idea of a concentration camp is excellent.'

According to Trotsky, Stalin quickly became accustomed to power and in the first months of the Revolution Lenin created the ruthless apparatus of state power that Stalin would later use to murder and enslave the Russian people. With little to

THE BREST-LITOVSK TREATY

On the day after the October Revolution, the Soviet government went to Germany with a peace plan. Negotiations began on 22 December in the city of Brest-Litovsk in Belarus. The Central Powers concluded a separate treaty with Ukraine on 9 February, but Leon Trotsky announced Russia's withdrawal from the talks on the following day. When the Germans resumed their military offensive, the Russians asked for the negotiations to begin again but the Germans responded with an ultimatum. The Russians must recommence the talks within two days and they had three further days in which to conclude them. Realizing that Russia was too weak to resist, Lenin threatened to resign if the treaty was not agreed so it was finally signed on 3 March and ratified by the Congress of Soviets on 15 March. As a result, Russia lost Ukraine, Finland and its Polish and Baltic territories. However, both the Ukrainian and the Russian treaties were nullified by the Armistice of 11 November 1918, when Germany conceded defeat in the First World War. Russia reoccupied Ukraine in 1919, during the Russian Civil War.

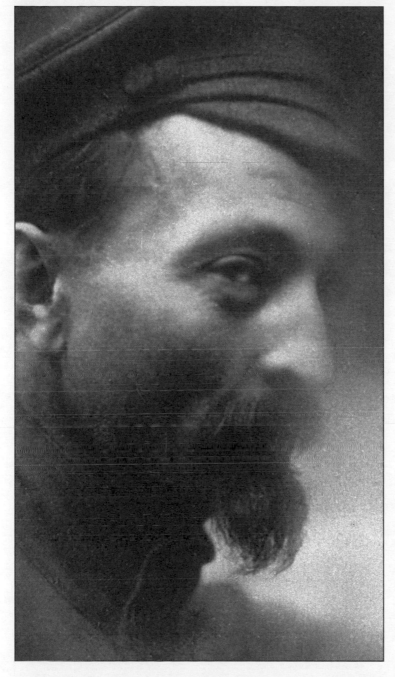

restrain them, the Cheka under Feliks Dzerzhinsky began the Red Terror, eliminating bourgeois 'class enemies' even when they had been loyal Communists. According to Dzerzhinsky, his Chekists were 'solid, hard men without pity who are ready to sacrifice everything for the sake of the Revolution'.

And his directive was chillingly simple.

'Just round up all the most resolute people you can who understand that there is nothing more effective than a bullet in the head to shut people up.'

Torture was now legalized and firing squads were commonplace. Live incineration was used and people were drowned after being flung from barges, or else simply hacked to bits. And the Cheka began building a network of concentration camps.

Dzerzhinsky did not beat about the bush: 'Round up people who understand there is nothing more effective than a bullet in the head to shut people up'

In the face of the German advance, Lenin and Trotsky signed the Brest-Litovsk Treaty which conceded the Baltic states and much of Ukraine to Germany in return for peace. Meanwhile, in Ukraine a White Volunteer Army was formed by the tsarist generals. They allied themselves with the Cossacks to the south and created a Czech Legion of 45,000 men by freeing Czech prisoners of war and anti-Bolshevik Russian officers in Siberia. Then they began advancing westwards. British Royal Marines occupied Murmansk to stop the port

Women sell sausages at Sukharevsky Market during the New Economic Policy in the 1920s. Under proposals by Lenin to stop the collapse of the Russian economy, some private ventures were allowed to make profits for individuals

falling into German hands and the besieged Soviet government withdrew inland to Moscow. In August, the British and the French, a number of Poles and a detachment of US Marines landed at Archangel to support the White Forces, while the Japanese landed in the east.

THE INVASION OF GEORGIA

After the Russian Revolution of 1917, the Democratic Republic of Georgia was established with a Menshevik government. Georgia was initially part of the Transcaucasian Federation, together with Armenia and Azerbaijan. When the Federation collapsed in May 1918, Georgia sought formal independence, which was recognized by a number of countries including Germany and Britain. However, its multi-party system was an anathema to the Bolsheviks. Without Lenin's approval the two leading Georgians in the Soviet regime – Stalin and Sergo Ordzhonikidze – ordered the Red Army to invade in February 1921. Georgia was then incorporated into the Transcaucasian Soviet Federated Socialist Republic, which signed a treaty with the Russian SFSR, Ukraine and Belarus to form the Soviet Union in December 1922. The Georgian Social Democrats organized a rebellion in 1924 which was brutally repressed by Stalin, who installed his fellow Georgian Lavrenty Beria as party chief. When Beria became head of the secret police in Moscow, Georgia was tightly controlled from the Kremlin.

Russian Civil War

Meanwhile, the Russian Civil War (1918–21) was raging. In May 1918, Lenin despatched Stalin to Tsaritsyn – later renamed Stalingrad, now Volgograd – as director-general of food supplies. Lenin ordered him to be ruthless.

'Be assured our hand will not tremble,' Stalin replied.

He immediately travelled south in an armoured train with 400 Red Guards and the teenage Nadya Alliluyev. Once in Tsaritsyn he assumed military powers and used the Cheka to purge the Bolshevik ranks of tsarists and 'counter-revolutionaries'. He was attempting to create a military force that would rival Trotsky's Red Army. Then he burned villages to intimidate the peasantry and deter bandit raids on food shipments.

On his return to Moscow in early 1919, Stalin married Nadya and moved into the Kremlin. Nadya worked as a typist in Lenin's office, providing Stalin with vital intelligence during Kremlin intrigues. In May 1919 Stalin was given a further assignment. He was sent to the Western Front, near Petrograd, where there had been mass desertions by Red Army soldiers. Stalin began by having deserters and renegades publicly executed as traitors but then he resumed his habit of persecuting his political allies. He arrested a group of Trotskyite 'military specialists' – former tsarist officers – and then put them in a barge on the Volga and sank it.

'Death solves all problems,' he said. 'No man, no problem.'

Even for Lenin this was a little harsh.

When Lavrenty Beria was appointed head of the secret police in Moscow by Stalin, Georgia was already very tightly controlled by the Kremlin

Stalin Tightens His Grip

Following the Bolshevik victory in the Russian Civil War, many members of
the government wanted to expand westwards, beginning with Poland. In May 1920,
Stalin was appointed as commissar to the South-Western Front after the Poles had

THE KREMLIN

In medieval Russia, most cities had a central fortress known as the Kremlin. The capitals of the old principalities were often built around their Kremlins, which usually contained an arsenal, administrative offices, a cathedral and palaces for bishops and princes. The most famous Kremlin is in Moscow. Built in the 12th century, it was the home of the central government of Russia from the 1620s until 1712, when Tsar Peter the Great moved the capital to St Petersburg. After 1918, the new Soviet government used the Kremlin as its headquarters. As well as being the seat of government it provided accommodation for those in power. After the fall of the Soviet Union in 1991, the Kremlin continued as the administrative centre of the Russian Federation.

Delegates of the plenipotentiary conference of representatives in Tbilisi in 1922: the Transcaucasian Federation became a 'founding member' of the USSR later that year. But how many of those pictured were members of Stalin's gangs?

taken Kiev. When he was ordered to retake Poland, he launched an attack on Lvov. However, Lenin and Trotsky wanted to subdue Warsaw instead. Stalin disagreed with them and refused to redirect his troops, after which the battles for both Warsaw and Lvov were lost. Stalin was blamed for the debacle and at the Ninth Party Congress on 22 September he was openly criticized by Trotsky.

Although Lenin and Stalin were committed Marxists, the fact that neither the workers nor the peasantry had supported the Bolsheviks during the Russian Civil War did not bother them. Lenin simply used it as an excuse to further centralize the Party structure. However, concessions had to be made. Lenin was forced to restore a degree of capitalism in order to save the regime and his New Economic Policy allowed small businesses and shops to operate for private profit. Otherwise he was unswerving in his policies. He employed show trials and executions in order to purge opposition both within the Party and outside it and he insisted on a Bolshevik dictatorship. This again provided Stalin with the perfect machine for repression when he took over. In 1922, Stalin was appointed general secretary of the Central Committee, which concentrated more power in his hands. By then, Georgia had seceded, so Stalin and his fellow Georgian Sergo Ordzhonikidze simply annexed it.

Lenin was appalled. He sought to establish a Union of Soviet Socialist Republics that was based on a federal system, rather than the unitary scheme that Stalin now sought to impose. But Lenin suffered the second of his three strokes in December 1922 and was forced into semi-retirement in his dacha outside Moscow. Stalin was a frequent visitor, but he fell out with Lenin's wife Krupskaya, warning her in typical Bolshevik fashion that if she did not fall into line the Central Committee would appoint Lenin a new wife. Lenin became increasingly suspicious of Stalin's overweening ambition and when he began writing his political testament he suggested that Stalin should be removed from his post as general secretary. Meanwhile Stalin was forging an alliance with Kamenev and Zinoviev against Trotsky, which prevented Lenin's testament from being read out at the Twelfth Party Congress in April 1923. It was then suppressed.

By then Lenin was powerless anyway, for in March 1923 he suffered his third major stroke, which deprived him of the power of speech. On the morning of 21 January 1924, Lenin died.

LENIN'S TESTAMENT

Between 23 and 26 December 1922, while recovering from a stroke, the ailing Lenin wrote a letter to be read out at a future Party Congress. It warned that Stalin was not cautious enough to be entrusted with the large amount of power he had accumulated. The biggest threat to the administration, Lenin wrote, was the strained relationship between Stalin and Trotsky, but Trotsky was too self-assured. And Bukharin might well be lauded as the Party's most eminent theoretician, but he had failed to master the dialectic. Lenin also declared that Kamenev and Zinoviev should not have been condemned for their actions in October 1917, when they had opposed the Bolshevik insurrection.

On 4 January 1923 Lenin added a post-script, suggesting that Stalin be removed from his post as general secretary. He had bungled the suppression of dissent in Georgia and he had also been rude to Krupskaya, Lenin's wife. On May 1924, a few days before the Thirteenth Party Congress, Krupskaya sent a copy to the Central Committee, which was already in Stalin's hands. He decreed that the testament could be read by the individual delegations but not by the assembled congress and he banned its publication. Stalin ensured that the document became a prohibited topic in the Soviet Union, though Krupskaya sent a copy to *The New York Times*, who printed it in its entirety.

CHAPTER SIX

SEIZING POWER

When Lenin died in 1924, Stalin set himself up as the high priest of the cult of the fallen leader. Russians had long worshipped their tsars and saints, after all. However, Stalin only promoted Lenin in this quasi-religious fashion so that he could follow in his footsteps and be venerated as a secular saint himself. Meanwhile, Stalin killed millions of people through the enforced collectivization of agriculture and the genocidal suppression of ethnic minorities.

Lenin's body lay in state for four days as 900,000 mourners filed by. Winston Churchill commented that Lenin's birth was Russia's greatest misfortune, but added that 'its next worst was Lenin's death'

O N 23 JANUARY 1924, TWO DAYS AFTER LENIN HAD DIED, STALIN LED A DELEGATION OF THE CENTRAL COMMITTEE TO COLLECT HIS BODY FROM HIS HOUSE IN GORKI. He then accompanied it on the train journey to the Paveletsky railway station in Moscow. From there, it was carried to the Hall of Columns in the House of Trade Unions, a handsome neoclassical building that was once a club for the Russian aristocracy. There Stalin stood in the guard of honour.

On the following day, at a memorial session of the Second Congress of Soviets, Stalin delivered the speech 'On the Death of Lenin' and vowed to fulfil the will of their fallen leader.

Lenin lay in state for four days while 900,000 mourners filed by. On the morning of 27 January Stalin once more became part of Lenin's guard of honour and at 9 am he helped carry Lenin's coffin out of the House of Trade Unions. Against the wishes of Lenin and his

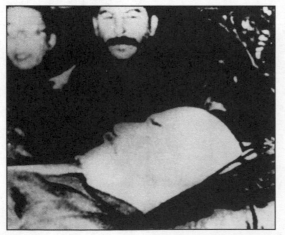

Stalin ensured that he was seen carrying Lenin's coffin; he was determined to inherit his mantle

widow, Nadezhda Krupskaya, Stalin had arranged a lavish funeral. He had also lied about the date so that Trotsky, Lenin's preferred successor, could not attend.

At 4 pm, after the day's ceremonies were over, Stalin helped lift the coffin once more and it was carried to the mausoleum on Red Square, where Lenin's body was to be embalmed and put on display. On 28 January Stalin eulogized Lenin in a speech he gave at the Kremlin Military School and on the following day he was elected to the Central Executive Committee of the Congress, when he directed a plenary session of the Central Committee of the Russian Communist Party. Finally, on 30 January, Stalin succeeded in being elected to the Presidium.

The Cult of Personality

Three days after Lenin's death, the city of Petrograd – now St Petersburg – was renamed Leningrad in his honour. Then on 10 April 1925 the city of Tsaritsyn – now Volgograd – was renamed Stalingrad. It was one of seven places in the Soviet Union that were named after Stalin. Later, towns in Albania, Bulgaria, East Germany, Hungary, Poland and Romania would also bear his name. Soon his image was everywhere. Huge portraits adorned public buildings and although he was only 5 foot 5 inches tall he was lent heroic stature by numerous statues in public squares. The annual Stalin Prize was instigated for achievements in the fields of mathematics, science, literature, architecture and the arts, and there was

The cult of Lenin was the basis for the cult of Stalin: here, railwaymen erect a Lenin monument in Tashkent

a Stalin Peace Prize that was often awarded to foreign dignitaries. Stalin himself was bestowed with such titles as 'Chief of Science', 'Brilliant Genius of Humanity', 'Father of Nations', 'Gardener of Human Happiness' and 'Great Architect of Communism'.

And history was rewritten in order to play up his role in the Revolution, as Soviet poet Yevgeny Yevtushenko relates.

'Stalin's name was indissolubly linked with Lenin's. Stalin knew how popular Lenin was and saw to it that history was rewritten in such a way as to make his own relations with Lenin seem much more friendly than they had been in fact. The rewriting was so thorough that perhaps Stalin himself believed his own version in the end.'

Even the dissident author of *Doctor Zhivago*, Boris Pasternak, fell for the trick by linking Stalin's name with Lenin's when he wrote,

This poster from 1943 proclaims, 'Stalin Leads us to Victory', as the Soviet leader adopts a Napoleonic pose

'Laughter in the village,
Voice behind the plough,
Lenin and Stalin,
And these verses now...'

After the Second World War – the Great Patriotic War – Stalin would be portrayed as the sole architect of victory, while the great commanders who actually won the battles, such as Marshal Zhukov, were sent off to obscure postings.

A 'Joseph Stalin' class of tank had been developed during the war and the battle cry of the Red Army was no longer 'For the Motherland' but 'For Stalin'. Stalin's name was even added to the Soviet national anthem, though it was removed after his death. Despite this orchestrated adulation, his successor Nikita Khrushchev recalled that Stalin had insisted that he should be remembered for 'the extraordinary modesty characteristic of truly great people'.

Soviet children were taught by their teachers to renounce their own parents, because Stalin was the father of them all. None of this was lost on Russian author

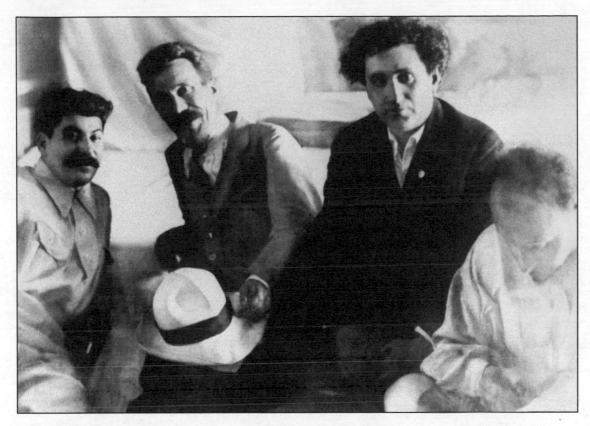

[From left to right] Stalin, Rykov, Zinoviev and Bukharin: if there was one thing nearly as bad as being Stalin's enemy, it was becoming a friend or ally. All three of the comrades here were tried and executed on Stalin's orders

A. O. Avdienko, who grovellingly wrote,

> *'I write books... All thanks to thee, O great educator, Stalin. I love a young woman with a renewed love and shall perpetuate myself in my children — all thanks to thee, great educator, Stalin. I shall be eternally happy and joyous, all thanks to thee, great educator, Stalin. Everything belongs to thee, chief of our great country. And when the woman I love presents me with a child the first word it shall utter will be: "Stalin." '*

With the support of Kamenev and Zinoviev, Stalin then ousted Trotsky, who had been seen as Lenin's heir apparent. After that he allied himself with Nikolay Bukharin and Aleksey Rykov, so that he could eject Kamenev and Zinoviev, and finally he forced out Bukharin and Rykov, which left him in complete control. He then went about creating what he called 'socialism in one country', thereby temporarily abandoning the Marxist concept of world revolution.

Collectivization

Not only did Stalin reject world revolution, he also abandoned Lenin's New Economic Policy. Private banks, peasant farms, retail shops and artisans' workshops

Kulaks are evicted from their smallholdings in Ukraine in the 1930s. Forced collectivization led to many kulaks destroying their tools or killing their animals rather than let them fall into the hands of the Soviets

were to be taken over by the state. Meanwhile Stalin pushed for the rapid industrialization and central control of the economy under a succession of five-year plans. All of this put a strain on food supplies and by the end of 1927 there was a critical shortage of grain. As a result Stalin called for the collectivization of agriculture. Twenty-five million rustic households would be forced into collective or state farms and those who resisted would either be dealt with by troops or the OGPU – the Unified State Political Directorate – that had replaced the Cheka. In January 1928, Stalin went to Siberia to oversee the confiscation of grain from the independent farmers who were accused of hoarding it. These smallholders, called *kulaks*, were now considered class enemies.

The Bolsheviks called a village farmer who owned more than 24 acres of land or employed farm workers a *kulak* – the Russian for 'fist'. Stalin saw them as the potential leaders of a future insurrection and in 1929 he proclaimed the policy of 'liquidating the *kulaks* as a class'. The OGPU, under their new chief Vyacheslav

NIKOLAY IVANOVICH BUKHARIN (1888–1938)

After studying economics at Moscow University, Bukharin joined the Russian Social-Democratic Workers' Party in 1906 and became a member of the Moscow Committee of the Bolshevik wing in 1908. Arrested and exiled, he escaped to Cracow where he worked with Lenin on the Party newspaper *Pravda*. In October 1916, he went to New York, where he edited the Leninist newspaper *Novy Mir* (New World) with Trotsky.

Following the February Revolution in 1917, Bukharin returned to Russia. After the October Revolution he joined the Central Committee and edited *Pravda*. He opposed the Brest-Litovsk Treaty because he thought that the war should be used as a springboard for a Communist revolution throughout Europe. A supporter of the New Economic Policy, he became a member of the Politburo after Lenin's death in 1924. Stalin used his support to undermine Kamenev and Zinoviev, and Bukharin replaced Zinoviev as chairman of the Comintern's executive committee in 1926.

But true to form Stalin turned on Bukharin in 1929, expelling him from the Comintern and the Politburo. Under pressure, Bukharin recanted his views and was appointed editor of the government newspaper *Izvestia* in 1934. In 1936, he helped write the Soviet Constitution but in the following year he was arrested and expelled from the Party for being 'Trotskyite'. A defendant in the last show trial of the Great Purge in March 1938, he was convicted of espionage and counter-revolutionary activities and executed. His wife was sent to a labour camp, but she survived to see her husband's reputation rehabilitated by the Soviet state under Mikhail Gorbachev in 1988.

ALEKSEY IVANOVICH RYKOV (1881–1938)

After joining the Russian Social-Democratic Workers' Party at the age of 18, Rykov went on to become a Bolshevik agitator. He participated in the 1905 Revolution, but after 1907 he attempted to engineer a reconciliation with the Mensheviks. When he returned to Russia after two years in Paris he was arrested and exiled.

Following the February Revolution in 1917, he advocated a coalition government, but when Lenin seized power he accepted the Bolshevik dictatorship and became People's Commissar of the Interior. In 1922 he joined the Politburo and became chairman of the Council of People's Commissars – that is, premier – in 1924.

A supporter of the New Economic Policy, he was stripped of his posts by Stalin in 1929–30, after being forced to recant. In 1937, he was expelled from the Party. Then in March 1938 he appeared in a show trial on a charge of treason and was sentenced to be executed. He was 'rehabilitated' in 1988.

Menzhinsky, was used to stir up hatred for the *kulaks*. Under the decree of 3 January 1930, 'On measures for the elimination of *kulak* households in districts of comprehensive collectivization', they were to be shot or imprisoned in the Gulag as decided by the OGPU, or exiled to Siberia, northern Russia, the Urals or Kazakhstan after their property had been confiscated. Otherwise they were evicted from their houses and used as forced labour within their own districts, which themselves became vast labour camps. Up to ten million *kulaks* were made homeless and it was against the law for anyone to help them.

Anyone opposing compulsory collectivization was denounced as a *kulak* and deported. Men and older boys, along with childless women and unmarried girls, became slave-labourers in Soviet mines and big industrial projects. Their holdings were absorbed into 240,000 collective farms and carts, livestock and farm implements would become the property of the state. The idea was that larger farms would be more efficient than smaller private holdings. But they were not and widespread famine was the result.

Once the bread basket of Russia, Ukraine was particularly hard hit. But the world knew little about it. In fact, *The New York Times*' Moscow correspondent Walter Duranty denied the very existence of the famine. His reporting won him the Pulitzer Prize in 1932, so it is small wonder that his reports were swallowed uncritically by such influential figures as George Bernard Shaw and H.G. Wells, who remained fans of Stalin. But others saw what was going on. When the writer Arthur Koestler visited Ukraine he looked out of his train and saw starving children who...

'... looked like embryos out of alcohol bottles... the stations were lined with begging peasants with swollen

VYACHESLAV RUDOLFOVICH MENZHINSKY (1874–1934)

The Polish–Russian nobleman and revolutionary Vyacheslav Menzhinsky joined the Russian Social-Democratic Workers' Party in 1902. After being arrested in 1905, he fled from Russia, returning in the summer of 1917. Following the October Revolution, he became People's Commissar of Finance and two years later he joined the Cheka, rising to become chairman of its successor the OGPU after Dzerzhinsky died in 1926.

Adept at counter-intelligence operations, he lured dissent writer Boris Savinkov and Britain's 'ace of spies' Sidney Reilly to Russia, where they were tortured and executed. Loyal to Stalin, Menzhinsky organized several important purges in 1930 and 1931, though he suffered from acute angina, which made it necessary to conduct his business from a couch in his office in the Lubyanka. He apparently died of natural causes in 1934 and was replaced by his deputy Genrikh Yagoda. When Yagoda was put on trial in 1938, he confessed to poisoning Menzhinsky, although the confession was obtained under duress.

hands and feet, the women holding up to the carriage windows horrible infants with enormous wobbling heads, sticklike limbs and swollen, pointed bellies'.

British journalist Malcolm Muggeridge, a Communist sympathizer, sent his reports back in the diplomatic bag to avoid the censor. His sense of shock permeates the following extract.

'The novelty of this particular famine, what made it so diabolical, was that it was not the result of some catastrophe like a drought or an epidemic. It was the deliberate creation of a bureaucratic mind which demanded the collectivization of agriculture... without any consideration whatever of the consequences in human suffering.'

In the Kiev region, a newly formed farm collective receives a deed for land tenure and pays obeisance to the generosity of Stalin. By 1932, 75 per cent of farms in Ukraine were forcibly collectivized – refuseniks were deported

Most workers continued to sow grain in Ukraine, but their harvest was exported abroad to provide money for Stalin's Five-Year Plan as well as to buy armaments for the USSR. People started starving to death, exactly as Stalin had planned

After the Bolshevik takeover in Russia in 1917, Ukraine had regained its independence, which had been lost in the 18th century, and a People's Republic was governed from Kiev, its ancient capital. But during the civil war between the tsarist Whites and the socialist Reds, the government in Moscow re-established control. By 1920, the Soviets had begun shipping huge amounts of grain out of Ukraine to feed the hungry people of the Russian cities. At the same time, a drought struck the territory.

In order to ameliorate the situation Lenin relaxed his grip on Ukraine, stopped taking so much grain and introduced his New Economic Policy, which allowed the free-market exchange of goods. This renewed Ukraine's interest in independence and led to a national revival in folk customs, the Ukrainian language, the arts, music and the orthodox religion.

When Lenin died in 1924, Stalin was determined to crush the burgeoning national revival movement, so he used the methods he had employed in the rest of the Soviet Union. Beginning in 1929, over 5,000 leading Ukrainians – scholars, scientists, cultural and religious leaders – were arrested and falsely accused of plotting an armed revolt. They were either shot without a trial or deported to prison camps in remote areas of Russia.

Stalin then ruthlessly imposed the Soviet system of collectivization on Ukrainian agriculture. All privately owned farmlands and livestock were to be seized by the state. However, some people resisted by burning down their homes or taking back their tools and farm animals from the collectives. Stalin could not tolerate such defiance so he sent troops to shoot down the protesting peasants and the secret police to wage a war of terror.

Nevertheless the people's resistance continued. Some peasants refused to work, leaving the wheat to rot in the fields. But Stalin would not relent. By mid-1932, nearly 75 per cent of the farms in Ukraine had been forcibly collectivized and on Stalin's orders the amount of foodstuffs to be shipped out to Russia was drastically increased. Even seed grain was confiscated from peasant households. Any man, woman or child caught taking even a handful of grain, now considered to be the property of the state, would be shot, deported or imprisoned for not less than ten years.

The Ukrainian Communists appealed to Moscow for a reduction in the grain quotas and the provision of emergency food aid, but Stalin's response was to denounce them and then send 100,000 loyal Russian soldiers to purge the Ukrainian Communist Party. Finally, the Soviets sealed off the borders of Ukraine in order to prevent any food entering the country and then Soviet police went from house to house seizing any remaining morsels. Starvation spread quickly. The most vulnerable members of the population, the elderly and the children, began dying of malnutrition. Some Ukrainians ate dogs, cats, frogs, mice, birds and leaves from the trees while others resorted to cannibalism, with parents sometimes even eating their own children.

LAZAR MOISEYEVICH KAGANOVITCH (1893–1991)

Kaganovitch was a young Jewish shoemaker when he joined the Bolshevik wing of the Russian Social-Democratic Workers' Party in 1911. He rose quickly through the ranks and by 1920 he was head of the Soviet government of Tashkent. In 1924 he was made head of Party patronage, in which capacity he helped Stalin defeat his political rivals. A keen supporter of collectivization, he boasted of killing 10,000 people a week in Ukraine. By 1930, he was a member of the Politburo, when he brought the Party in Moscow under Stalin's control, helped build the subway and supervised the distribution of heavy farm equipment to shore up the failing collective system. He also supplied the labour to build the White Sea–Baltic Canal.

He occupied a number of positions in central government before becoming deputy premier in 1938 and he became a member of the war cabinet. After the war he was one of the few Jews to be spared during Stalin's post-war persecution. Under Khrushchev he opposed de-Stalinization and in 1957 he was removed from government. He was expelled from the Party in the early 1960s.

Sometimes mothers would toss their emaciated children on to passing railroad cars in the hope that someone would take pity on them and give them a home. But in Kiev, Lvov, Kharkov and Odessa people were dropping dead in the streets and their bodies were being dumped in mass graves. At times people were carted away and buried while they were still alive. The death toll from the 1932–33 famine in Ukraine alone has been conservatively estimated at between six and seven million – 25,000 people were dying every day.

According to one Soviet author, 'The first who died were the men. Later on the children. And last of all the women. But before they died, people often lost their senses and ceased to be human beings.'

Party activists continued confiscating grain even as whole villages perished. As one of them, Victor Kravchenko, wrote,

'On a battlefield men die quickly, they fight back, they are sustained by fellowship and a sense of duty. Here I saw people dying in solitude by slow degrees, dying hideously, without the excuse of sacrifice for a cause. The most terrifying sights were the little children with skeleton limbs dangling from balloon-like abdomens. Starvation had wiped every trace of youth from their faces, turning them into tortured gargoyles; only in their eyes still lingered the reminder of childhood.'

Yet in 1933, with Soviet granaries bursting, another of Stalin's lieutenants, Mendel Khataevich, declared the famine a great success.

'It took a famine to show the peasants who is the master here,' he said. 'It cost millions of lives, but the collective farm system is here to stay.'

The famine in Ukraine is now seen as genocide and it is called the *Holodomor* – the Ukrainian word for 'murder by hunger'. Estimates of how many died as a result of collectivization vary. The Russian novelist Aleksandr Solzhenitsyn, author of *The Gulag Archipelago*, claimed that 60 million people perished, while Soviet figures put the death toll as low as 700,000. However, it is generally reckoned that at least ten million men, women and children died.

Stalin sent three of his most ruthless commissars – Molotov, Kaganovitch and Yagoda – to crush the last remnants of opposition, for in some places peasants defended themselves with shotguns and pitchforks, or deliberately destroyed the livestock, particularly the horses needed for ploughing. For their part, the peasants saw collectivization as a return to serfdom, which had been abolished by Tsar Alexander II in 1861.

Tanks were brought in and machine guns cut down those who resisted, while churches were sacked and monks and nuns were deported. A court in Kharkov handed down 1,500 death sentences in a single day. One woman was sentenced to ten years' detention for cutting a hundred ears of corn in her own plot, two weeks after her husband had starved to death. Peasants who were not starved or shot were summarily deported to the labour camps that fed the construction of the White Sea–Baltic Canal or the gold mines at Magadan in the east.

Those who carried out these atrocities were unconcerned. Young Communist activist Lev Kopolev, who scoured the countryside for hidden stores of grain, wrote a blithe account of his heartless activities.

> 'I saw women and children with distended bellies turning blue, with vacant eyes and corpses in ragged sheepskin coats and cheap felt-booted corpses in peasant huts, in the snow of old Vologoda, under the bridges of Kharkov...'

But he managed to justify the suffering he had seen.

> 'We were realizing historical necessity. We were performing our revolutionary duty. We were obtaining grain for the socialist fatherland... I emptied out the old folks' storage chests, stopping my ears to the children's crying and women's wails... I was convinced I was accomplishing the great and necessary transformation of the countryside.'

He was, of course, operating under Stalin's orders.

Some party activists did rebel though. A small bunch of Bolsheviks called for the liquidation of Stalin and his clique but they were rounded up and sent to the Gulag. By March 1930 approximately 58 per cent of peasant households had been absorbed into collective farms. This figure had risen dramatically from four per cent in October 1929 and 21 per cent in January 1930. However, so many peasants had slaughtered their livestock and smashed their equipment that Stalin decided to slow down the collectivization process. The Russian people's hostility against the regime also grew, so on 2 March 1930 Stalin published an article called 'Dizzy from Success', in which he shifted the blame for the excesses on to local officials, who had 'lost clearness of mind'. Many peasants took this as a signal to leave the collective farms, with only 24 per cent remaining by June. In the fertile 'black earth' region of the south-west the number of people living on collective farms dropped from 82 per cent in March to 18 per cent in May.

Nevertheless, Stalin was hell-bent on extracting large amounts of agricultural products from the Russian countryside. These were dumped on to foreign markets in order to generate the cash needed to finance his massive military build-up and his Five-Year Plan for the modernization of the Soviet Union.

That autumn the collectivization process began all over again. By 1937, 93 per cent of peasant households were back on collective farms and working for the state. Despite the millions of deaths that resulted from forced collectivization, it established Soviet power in the countryside. As part of the state-controlled economy, it provided the capital needed for Stalin to transform the Soviet Union into a major industrial power.

Lysenkoism

During the Great Famine, Stalin turned to a previously unknown agronomist, Trofim Benisovich Lysenko (1898–1976), who was the scion of a peasant family and an ardent Leninist. In 1928, Lysenko claimed to have developed an agricultural technique that would treble or quadruple yields by exposing wheat seed to high humidity and low temperature. The seed would even germinate in snow-covered fields, he asserted.

In fact, the technique, known as vernalization, was not new – it had been known since 1854 – and it did not produce the yields Lysenko promised. However, Lysenko was one of the few agronomists who supported collectivization and while other biologists were conducting heredity experiments using fruit flies he at least was studying cereal production. He was hailed as a genius, a scientist who came up with solutions to practical problems. While he was happy to denounce other biologists as 'fly lovers and people haters', the Soviet propaganda machine overstated his successes and avoided any mention of his failures.

Lysenko claimed that vernalization increased wheat yields by 15 per cent, but his findings were solely based upon questionnaires given to farmers. The truth was that his claim that his 'new' methods would create an 'agricultural revolution' had merely encouraged peasants to plant more wheat. Nevertheless, he had managed to motivate the peasants and he was promoted by Stalin. Other biologists were, by comparison, considered 'wreckers', because they refused to apply their science to the Soviet economy and their methods, particularly the study of genetics, were seen as inherently 'bourgeois', if not 'fascist'.

On the other hand, Lysenko rejected orthodox genetics by maintaining that evolution was instead based on the inheritability of acquired characteristics. This concept was central to the framework of agricultural theories that became known as 'Lysenkoism'. Scientists who opposed Lysenko's ideas were arrested, imprisoned, executed or sent to labour camps. In 1948 genetics was officially declared a 'bourgeois pseudoscience' and research was discontinued. Lysenkoism continued under Khruschev, who fancied himself an agricultural expert.

During his career, Lysenko held senior positions in the Ukraine All-Union Institute of Selection and Genetics in Odessa (1929–38) and the Institute of Genetics of the Academy of Sciences of the USSR (1940–65). After a debate at the V.I. Lenin All-Union Academy of Agricultural Sciences, the Central Committee of the Communist Party directed that all textbooks and courses be changed in accordance with Lysenko's views. In 1964 Lysenko was denounced as a charlatan after an official investigation of his records.

Konstantin Pysin, the USSR deputy agriculture minister [left], hands Trofim Lysenko an award for services to agriculture: Lysenko claimed to have invented a technique for increasing wheat yields, but he was a charlatan

CHAPTER SEVEN

THE GROWTH OF THE GULAG

Under Stalin a vast network of slave-labour camps grew up. They were run by a division of the OGPU called the *Glavnoye Upravlyeniye Ispravityel'no-Trudovih Lagyeryey*, or 'Chief Administration of Corrective Labour Camps', which is better known as 'Gulag', its acronym. The term 'Gulag' is also used to describe the entire Soviet labour camp network or an individual camp. The camp inmates were left to the tender mercies of Leonid Zakovsky, the author of a handbook on torture.

WHEN THE BOLSHEVIKS CAME TO POWER IN 1917, THERE WERE 28,600 PEOPLE IN THE PENAL SYSTEM. Most of them were released because even common thieves were considered political prisoners. It was thought that the capitalist system had forced them into a life of crime. However, it soon became clear that order had to be re-imposed.

In December 1917, Feliks Dzerzhinsky became head of the newly-formed Cheka. He began by rounding up anyone he considered to be 'enemies of the people'. They were herded into barracks, factories and the homes of the dispossessed gentry, to be shot in their basements. A decree of 15 April 1919 set up a system of forced labour camps to house corrupt officials, embezzlers, aristocrats, saboteurs, businessmen, landowners, aristocrats and dissidents. Their numbers were swelled with prisoners from the Russian Civil War. Other people were imprisoned for simply showing 'individualistic tendencies' – a crime in a collectivist society – while artists and writers were sent to the Gulag if their work did not conform to the doctrine of 'Socialist Realism', as decreed by Stalin. People who had lived abroad or who had relatives living outside the Soviet Union were also liable to imprisonment.

The Ayach-Yaginsk mine barracks in Arctic Vorkuta, some 1,100 miles (1,800 kilometres) north-east of Moscow: it's been estimated that more than 20 million perished in the terrible conditions of Soviet labour camps

SOCIALIST REALISM

Art appeared in wide variety after the 1917 Revolution, but in 1932 it was decided that it had to be subordinated to the needs and dictates of the Party. Over the next two years, the Central Committee disbanded all existing artistic organizations and in 1934 the First All-Union Congress of Soviet Writers proclaimed that 'Socialist Realism' – the depiction of heroic working people in their 'revolutionary development' – was the approved method for Soviet artists. Stalin's mouthpiece on cultural matters, Andrei Zhdanov [*pictured above, left, with writer Maxim Gorky*], told the congress that henceforth the artist was to be the 'engineer of the human soul'. Campaigns against 'formalism' and 'intuitivism' were launched in *Pravda*, resulting in show trials in 1936. There was a second cultural purge in 1946, this time against non-Russian works. The paintings of the French impressionists were removed from galleries and museums and the works of Jewish artists – considered 'rootless cosmopolitans' – were also suppressed. Even approved 'Social Realist' artists were condemned if foreign influences were detected in their work. After Stalin's death in 1953, and his repudiation by Khrushchev in 1956, artistic freedom began to reassert itself.

By the late 1920s, 300 labour camps contained a total of around 100,000 prisoners. Once Stalin was in power the camps were sources of cheap labour rather than being rehabilitation centres for deviant socialists but the fiction of 'corrective labour' persisted. In 1927 an official in charge of prison administration wrote,

'The exploitation of prison labour, the system of squeezing "golden sweat" from them, the organization of production in places of confinement, which while profitable from a commercial point of view is fundamentally lacking in corrective significance — these are entirely inadmissible in Soviet places of confinement.'

Along with prisons in Moscow and Leningrad and ten small camps designed for the most dangerous prisoners, the GPU/OGPU built a series of 'Northern Special Purpose Camps' around a disused monastery on the Solovetsky Islands in the White Sea and on the mainland near Archangel. There the inmates were forced to work in appalling conditions, while ostensibly playing their part in the fulfilment of the economic goals of socialism. This was the beginning of the Gulag. A tightening of the penal code had brought about a significant growth in the population of these prison camps, mainly because of an ever-growing demand for labour. Thousands of workers were needed for large-scale projects such as the construction of the 141-mile-long White Sea–Baltic Canal, for instance, which took only 20 months to complete. It was built almost entirely by labourers using primitive pickaxes, shovels and makeshift wheelbarrows. Over 100,000 convicts died during its construction, though estimates vary. The use of convict labour was not publicized at the time though the construction of the canal was hailed as a great triumph of socialist endeavour. Celebratory books were released in both the Soviet Union and the United States, along with the documentary film *Baltic to White Sea Waterway*. However, the canal eventually turned out to be too narrow and shallow to carry most sea vessels.

THE PERM GULAG

During the late 1940s, some 150,000 inmates were imprisoned in more than 150 camps around the city of Perm, near the Urals. They made up around one-third of the total workforce of the area. In 1946, Perm 36 – a camp that was also known at ITK-6 – was built there in a forested area near the border with Siberia. There were four barracks each holding 250 prisoners, a punishment block, an outhouse, a prison hospital and a headquarters building.

The prisoners were woken at 6 am and then they would be given a meagre breakfast at 6.30 am before roll-call at 7 am. At 7.30 am they would set off into the forest under armed escort, a march that took one and a half hours. Then they would begin their day's work, which was felling trees with simple frame saws. This back-breaking work would end at 6 pm. There would then be another one and a half hour march back to the camp. After dinner at 7.30 pm the prisoners had to spend three hours on camp duties, such as chopping firewood, shovelling snow, gardening and repairing roads, before lights out at 11 pm. Tree felling continued all the year round. When the spring thaw came, the lumber would be sent downriver to help rebuild the Soviet cities that had been damaged during the Second World War.

Life in the Gulag

Life in a typical Gulag was physically exhausting for the prisoners, who were forced to work for up to 14 hours a day. Often toiling in the most extreme climates, they

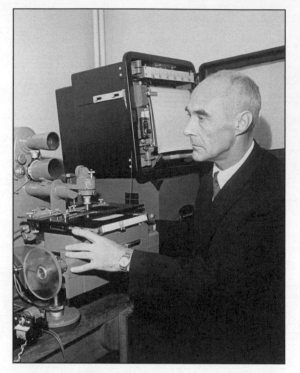

Soviet astronomer and astrophysicist Kozyrev found himself among distinguished company in the labour camp

spent their days felling trees with handsaws and axes or digging the frozen ground with the most rudimentary implements.

After 11½ hours of toil – not including the time it took to be assigned a task, collect the tools and return them – Professor Nikolai Kozyrev, formerly director of research at the Pulkovo Space Observatory in Leningrad, was driven to make an observation.

'How far man is still from perfection. Just think how many people and what minds are needed to do the job of one horse.'

He had been hauling logs with Professor Epifanov, professor of Marxism-Leninism at the Academy of Mining in Moscow; Colonel Ivanov, an erstwhile hero of the Red Army; and Jacques Rossi, a secret agent of the Comintern.

Others mined coal or copper by hand, often suffering painful and frequently fatal lung diseases from the inhalation of dust and ore. In a Gulag mine, an inmate's production quota could be as high as 13,000 kg (nearly 13 tons) of ore a day. Failure to meet that quota would result in a cut in rations and the prisoner would then succumb to malnutrition. As it was, the daily ration of a chunk of bread and a bowl of soup was barely enough to survive on. The bowls and other utensils were made in the camp workshops by prisoners who exchanged them for food.

According to Russian author Varlam Shalamov who spent 20 years in a Gulag,

'Each time they brought in the soup... it made us all want to cry. We were ready to cry for fear that the soup would be thin. And when a miracle occurred and the soup was thick we couldn't believe it and ate it as slowly as possible. But even with thick soup in a warm stomach there remained a sucking pain; we'd been hungry for too long.'

The procurator of the Soviet Union, Andrei Vyshinksy, wrote to NKVD chief Nikolay Yezhov in 1938, saying,

'Among the prisoners there are some so ragged and lice-ridden that they pose a sanitary danger to the rest. These prisoners have deteriorated to the point of losing any

resemblance to human beings. Lacking food... they collect refuse and, according to some prisoners, eat rats and dogs.'

According to Shalamov,

'All human emotions — love, friendship, envy, concern for one's fellow man, compassion, longing for fame, honesty — had left us with the flesh that had melted from our bodies.'

The lack of vitamins in the diet brought scurvy and other diseases, there was no medical treatment and the inmates' clothing was barely adequate. The largest camps lay in the most extreme geographical and climatic regions, ranging from the Arctic north to eastern Siberia and the searing steppes of Kazakhstan. In the Arctic regions prisoners froze to death, a fate often shared by the guards and their dogs. There was no hope of escape. Even so, the guards had every reason to be vigilant. If a prisoner attempted to abscond on his watch, a guard could be stripped of his uniform and become a prisoner himself.

During their non-working hours the prisoners were confined to a compound surrounded by a barbed-wire fence and overlooked by armed guards in watchtowers. They lived in overcrowded, stinking, poorly heated barracks. For punishment there were solitary confinement cells where prisoners slept on bare planking. They were unheated and some of them were so shallow that it was impossible to stand up. There were also summary executions. Prisoners could be shot for 'continuing anti-Soviet activity during imprisonment' under NKVD Order Number 00447. Tens of thousands suffered this fate.

Despite the cold, prisoners were subjected to regular strip searches, often just to humiliate them. It also gave the guards a chance to steal anything valuable, such as sweaters, mittens, socks, scarves, vests and shoes. Women were often raped by the guards, prison employees or other prisoners. Some became pregnant and others were pregnant on arrival. Occasionally, the Gulag authorities released pregnant women and women with young children under special amnesties, but mothers were usually forced to return to work after giving birth. Their babies were then placed in special orphanages. Often mothers could not find their children after leaving the camps.

Violence among the prisoners was commonplace as they competed for life's necessities. Political prisoners were mixed in with ordinary criminals – murderers, rapists and thieves. They also had to endure the arbitrary violence of the camp guards. And everywhere there were informers. Fellow prisoners were always looking for a minor infraction that could be reported to the Gulag authorities.

The name Kolyma struck fear into even the most hardened inmates. Reputedly

Even though Stalin was a shameless dictator, the Soviet Union maintained the fiction that it was a democracy. Elections were held, but the name of only one Communist Party candidate appeared on the ballot paper for each office. The turnout was high even so, because people feared being punished if they did not go through the farce of 'voting'. In 1949, a beekeeper named Ivan Burylov protested against this absurd ritual by writing the word 'comedy' on his ballot paper. Even though the ballot was supposed to be secret, the Soviet authorities linked the defaced ballot paper to Burylov. He was sentenced to eight years in the Gulag for this heinous crime.

the coldest inhabited place on the planet, prisoners said that at Kolyma there were 12 months of winter: the rest of the year was summer. Temperatures reached minus 90 degrees C (minus 130 degrees F). Kolyma was so remote that it could not be reached overland. Prisoners were transported across the entire length of the Soviet Union by rail before spending months on the Pacific coast waiting for the waterways to be free of ice. They were put on ships that sailed past Japan and up the Kolyma River and then put to work in the gold mines. Thirty per cent of the prisoners died there each year.

Getting There

Even the most trivial offences could result in a trip to the Gulag. The penalty for arriving late for work on three separate occasions was three years in a labour camp. Petty theft, such as stealing potatoes left in a field after the harvest, even though you were starving, attracted a ten-year sentence and making a joke about a Communist Party official could mean a stay of up to 25 years. Sentences could be arbitrarily extended and former inmates were forced to live near the camps even when they were released. It could be years before they were allowed to return home – if at all.

Prisoners filled the Gulag in five major waves. The first was in 1929 to 1932, during the collectivization period, and the figures rose again in 1934, when Stalin extended Article 58 of the Soviet Criminal Code to include various 'counter-revolutionary activities'. Stalin's Great Purge – or Terror – of 1936 to 1938 filled the Gulag once more and in 1939 and 1940 hundreds of thousands of people from the eastern half of Poland, the Baltic states and other territories occupied by the Soviet Union were sent there.

The Gulag emptied a little during the Second World War, when many of the prisoners were sent to fight on the front lines, often in penal battalions. For those who remained, conditions worsened. Work quotas were increased, rations were cut and medical supplies were diverted to the front, leading to a sharp increase in mortality. During the winter of 1941 a quarter of the population of the Gulag died from starvation and by 1943 over half a million people had perished.

With the coming of peace, the number of inmates swelled again. Some were deserters or war criminals. Soviet prisoners of war repatriated from German prisoner of war camps were often sent directly to the Gulag. By not laying down their lives for the motherland they were seen as anti-Soviet. They were even accused of treason for 'co-operating with the enemy'. At the very least they had been contaminated by coming into contact with the world outside the Soviet Union, no matter how harsh it was.

ARTICLE 58

Article 58 of the Penal Code of the Russian Soviet Federative Socialist Republic, which allowed the arrest of anyone suspected of counter-revolutionary activities, went into force on 25 February 1927. It was updated on 8 June 1934 with a series of sub-clauses that gave Stalin new powers to use against anyone he deemed 'counter-revolutionary'.

• **Article 58-1** defined counter-revolutionary activity as 'any action aimed at overthrowing, undermining or weakening of the power of workers' and peasants' Soviets… and governments of the USSR and Soviet and autonomous republics, or at the undermining or weakening of the external security of the USSR and main economical, political and national achievements of the proletarial revolution.

This was not limited to anti-Soviet acts because it also prohibited conduct that undermined the 'international solidarity of workers' in any other 'workers' state'.

• **Article 58-2** prohibited any armed uprising or intervention that aimed to seize power as the Bolsheviks had done. The punishment was imprisonment or death, with the confiscation of property and the formal recognition of an offender as an 'enemy of workers'.

• **Article 58-3** forbade Russians to contact foreigners 'with counter-revolutionary purposes' – that is, any foreigners at all. Punishment was as Article 58-2.

• **Article 58-4** banned citizens from giving any kind of help to the 'international bourgeoisie', which did not recognize the equality of the communist political system and so strove to overthrow it. Punishment was as Article 58-2.

• **Article 58-5** made it an offence to urge any foreign entity into breaking diplomatic relations or breaking international treaties or into a declaration of war, military intervention, blockade, capture of state property, or other aggressive actions against the USSR.

• **Article 58-6** banned espionage.

• **Article 58-7** outlawed the undermining of state industry, transport, monetary circulation or the credit system, as well as co-operative societies and organizations, with counter-revolutionary purpose. Offenders were called 'wreckers'.

- **Article 58-8** banned terrorist acts against representatives of Soviet power or of workers' and peasants' organizations.

- **Article 58-9** prohibited the damaging of transport, communications, water supplies, warehouses and other buildings or state and communal property with counter-revolutionary purposes.

- **Article 58-10** banned anti-Soviet and counter-revolutionary propaganda and agitation. The punishment was at least six months of imprisonment or, in times of unrest or war, the same as 58.2.

- **Article 58-11** made it an offence to furnish any kind of organizational assistance or support in relation to the preparation or execution of the above crimes.

- **Article 58-12** punished the non-reporting of counter-revolutionary activity with at least six months' imprisonment.

- **Article 58-13** belatedly banned the active struggle against the revolutionary movement by tsarist personnel and members of 'counter-revolutionary governments' during the Russian Civil War.

- **Article 58-14** was added on 6 June 1937. It banned 'counter-revolutionary sabotage' – that is, conscious non-execution or deliberately careless execution of 'defined duties', aimed at the weakening of the power of the government and of the functioning of the state apparatus. Punishment was at least one year's imprisonment, rising to execution by firing squad and confiscation of property. The punishments for all of the other offences, unless otherwise stated, were as 58.2.

Article 58 gave the secret police *carte blanche* to arrest and imprison anyone they found suspicious. Sentences could be as long as 25 years. Needless to say, the Gulag soon filled up. Russians who had been held as prisoners of war by the enemy during the Second World War were also imprisoned. Article 58 also applied to the Soviet zone of occupation in Germany. Anyone who had any contact with the West could be sent to a Gulag for an indefinite period.

The Post-war Gulag

Under an agreement made with their wartime Allies at Yalta in February 1945, Britain and the United States were obliged to repatriate over two million former citizens of the Soviet Union. Some of them – notably Cossacks – had escaped decades before, following the Russian Civil War, and had become the citizens of

Khrushchev shocked delegates at the Twentieth Congress of the CPSU, or Central Committee, in 1956 by denouncing the personality cult of Stalin. 'It was wrong to elevate a single individual to the status of near-god'

other countries. They too went to the Gulag. These forced repatriations went on until as late as 1947.

Large numbers of people from territory that had been occupied or annexed by the Soviet Union after the war were also imprisoned. Even the survivors of Nazi concentration camps were transported directly into the Gulag on the grounds that they could only have survived if they had collaborated. Sometimes, the Russian authorities were even spared the cost of building labour camps. If Nazi concentration camps were in good order when they were taken over by the Russians, it was simply a question of removing the Nazi insignia and replacing them with Soviet ones. Buchenwald and Sachsenhausen were turned into NKVD 'special camps', for instance.

Estimates vary about how many people disappeared into the Gulag. There were hundreds of camps, each holding from two to ten thousand prisoners. By the 1950s, it is estimated that there were around two and a half million people in the Gulag. In 1989 a group of Soviet historians examined the records of the Gulag administration and came to the conclusion that a total of ten million people were sent to the camps between 1934 and 1947. Solzhenitsyn reckoned that between 1928 and 1953 'some forty to fifty million people had served long sentences in the Archipelago'. Harsh climatic conditions, inadequate food, disease and summary execution killed off at least ten per cent of the inmates and Western scholars estimate that from 1918 to 1956 between 15 and 30 million people died. But this did not matter to the authorities – there were always new prisoners to replace those who had perished. The graves of the dead were identified by simple markers that did not carry their names, just their prison numbers.

The Gulag system continued for some time after the death of Stalin in 1953. However, the Soviet state began to release its political prisoners in the following year. A trickle became a deluge after Nikita Khrushchev denounced Stalin and Stalinism in a speech to the Twentieth Congress of the Communist Party of the Soviet Union in February 1956. By the end of the 1950s, virtually all 'corrective labour colonies' had disappeared, though some camps were maintained in Soviet satellites such as Poland, Czechoslovakia and Mongolia. With the gradual collapse of Communism, these also disappeared.

Was Stalin's Wife Murdered?

While Stalin was building the Gulag that would turn the Soviet Union into a slave state, he suffered a personal tragedy when his second wife Nadezhda Sergeevna Alliluyeva (Nadya) committed suicide. Many people believe that he was responsible.

Married in 1919, the couple had two children, Vasily and Svetlana. According to Nadya's good friend Polina Molotova, she and Stalin constantly fought. As a committed Communist, Nadya was upset by the news of the famine in Ukraine. She also suspected Stalin of having numerous affairs, which is more than likely because Stalin considered the wives of comrades and Kremlin staff to be fair game. At the time of her suicide she believed that he was having an affair with her hairdresser.

On the evening of 8 November 1932, there was a party at the Kremlin to celebrate the 15th anniversary of the Revolution. Stalin began flirting with 34-year-old actress Galya Yegorova, the wife of a Red Army commander, who was well known for her risqué dresses and her many affairs. Understandably, Nadya grew annoyed. Stalin then upbraided her for not raising her glass in a toast. Some say that he tossed orange peel at her, while others maintain that he flicked cigarettes at her from across the dinner table.

'Hey, you! Have a drink!' he shouted.

'My name isn't "Hey"!' she replied angrily, then she stormed out of the room. Polina followed her and calmed her down.

While Nadya went back to their apartment in the Kremlin, Stalin went to a dacha with a woman, probably Galya Yegorova. No one knows what time he returned. In the morning, Nadya was found shot dead. Next to her body was a pistol that had been bought for her by her brother Pavel. It was assumed that she had committed suicide. However, rumours soon spread that Stalin had returned early, the couple had rowed and Nadya had been murdered.

Nadya's death 'altered history', said Stalin's nephew Leonid Redens. 'It made the Terror inevitable.'

According to an official announcement Nadya had died from appendicitis, but two doctors refused to sign a death certificate to that effect. They were convicted and executed during the Terror. Polina Molotova also disappeared into the Gulag. Meanwhile, Stalin consoled himself with Pavel's wife Zhenya, his sister-in-law. When Pavel died – after perhaps being poisoned by Beria – Stalin sent Beria to propose that Zhenya become Stalin's 'housekeeper'. Zhenya was afraid that Beria might accuse her of trying to poison Stalin, so she married an old friend. Stalin remarked that it was indecent to remarry so soon after the death of Pavel and

Stalin and wife Nadezhda Alliluyeva [in the foreground] picnic with friends in a wood near Moscow

Beria accused her of poisoning her husband so that she could marry her lover. But luckily for Zhenya Stalin found another housekeeper, a young, submissive peasant girl named Valentina Vasilevna Istomina ('Valechka') who stayed with him for the next 18 years.

THE *SUKA* WARS (BITCH WARS)

The Russian word *suka* merely means 'bitch' in English, but in Russian criminal argot it refers to someone who has co-operated with the law enforcement authorities or the government. The English counterpart is a 'snitch' or a 'rat'. Within the prison system, those who collaborated with the authorities were the lowest of the low and *sukas* had a particularly miserable life in prisons. The *Suka* Wars (Bitch Wars) took place within the Soviet prison system between 1945 and some time around the death of Joseph Stalin in 1953. During the Great Patriotic War, Stalin told prisoners that in exchange for fighting in the Red Army they would be granted a pardon at the end of the war. However, Stalin reneged on his promise and sent those who had served in the military back to prison. There they were declared *sukas*. They were forced to collaborate with the prison officers in order to survive. In return, they got some of the better jobs in the prisons. This set them at odds with the regular criminals and a conflict broke out between those who had served in the military and prisoners who were part of the Russian criminal underground. The prison authorities turned a blind eye, because they had little interest in keeping the inmates alive.

CHAPTER EIGHT

THE TERROR

Some members of the Communist Party opposed collectivization and called for the removal of Stalin, but he would countenance no opposition. His plan was to build a state apparatus that would suppress any rivals. All heretical Marxists, including Lenin's entire Politburo, would be shot. With the aid of a series of show trials and extra-judicial killings, he purged the Communist Party and filled the population with terror.

I N THE SUMMER OF **1933**, THE HEALTH OF THE CHAIRMAN OF THE **OGPU**, VYACHESLAV MENZHINSKY, WENT INTO DECLINE AND HE DIED OF WHAT WAS SAID TO BE KIDNEY AND HEART DISEASE. His deputy Genrikh Yagoda took his place. While it was generally felt that the OGPU had done a good job by enforcing collectivization, liquidating the *kulaks* and creating the Gulag, Stalin decided that he needed an effective instrument of repression closer to home. Accordingly, Yagoda was also put in charge of the MVD – the Ministry of Internal Affairs. The OGPU and the MVD were then merged to form the NKVD or *Narodnyi Kommissariat Vnutrennikh Del* (People's Commissariat for Internal Affairs). This gave Yagoda control of the regular police force as well as the secret police, together with unprecedented powers.

Stalin needed the support of powerful and ultra-loyal supporters like Yagoda, because he had enemies within the fold. Their leader was Martemyan Ryutin, a disaffected member of the Central Committee. He had been an ally to Bukharin and

GENRIKH GRIGORYEVICH YAGODA
(1891–1938)

Born into the family of a Jewish watchmaker, he became a Bolshevik in 1907. After the October Revolution he joined the Cheka, which became the OGPU in 1924, and he was one of the founders of the Gulag. When his chief at the OGPU, Vyacheslav Menzhinsky, conveniently died (it was later said that Yagoda poisoned him) Yagoda took his place.

In 1934 Yagoda was put in charge of Stalin's new People's Commissariat for Internal Affairs, or the NKVD. Under Yagoda, even children were arrested for 'stealing Socialist property' and sent to labour camps. A notorious killer, Yagoda was almost certainly responsible for the murder of Leningrad Party secretary Sergey Kirov, on Stalin's behalf. He then organized the first show trial of the Great Purge, which led to the executions of Kamenev and Zinoviev. In the following year, he became a victim of the Great

Purge himself. Arrested in 1937, he was immediately accused of being a 'Trotskyite' saboteur.

During his last days at the Lubyanka prison, he told his interrogator Abram Slutsky, 'From Stalin I deserved nothing but gratitude for my faithful service; from God I deserved the most severe punishment for having violated his commandments thousands of times. Now look where I am and judge for yourself: is there a God, or not...'

According to Aleksandr Solzhenitsyn, Yagoda believed that Stalin would save him. During the show trial itself he appealed to him directly for mercy.

'I appeal to you,' he said. 'For you I built two great canals.'

At that moment a match flared in the shadows behind a muslin curtain and the outline of a pipe could be seen. Yagoda was sentenced to death and was shot soon afterwards.

No laughing matter: Khrushchev with the murderous Yagoda [centre] during the construction of the Moscow–Volga canal. The waterway was built between 1932 and 1937 by Gulag prisoners – many were executed once the task was complete

Rykov. When they were eased out, he was expelled from the Party and arrested. But after his release he was allowed to rejoin.

In June 1932, Ryutin secretly circulated a 200-page document called 'Stalin and the Crisis of the Proletarian Dictatorship'. It claimed to be the manifesto of the League of Marxist-Leninists and it was also known as the 'Ryutin platform'. The document called Stalin 'the evil genius of the Revolution'. While bringing terror and lawlessness to the countryside, it went on to say, Stalin had reduced the press to a 'monstrous factory of lies'. The author demanded that Trotsky be readmitted to the Party and concluded that 'Stalin and his clique will not and cannot voluntarily give up their position, so they must be removed by force.'

On 23 September 1932, Ryutin was identified as the author of the document and arrested. Ten days later, a group of people close to Ryutin, known as the 'Ryutin group', were expelled from the Communist Party, and the document itself was completely suppressed – only a single typed copy remained in the secret police archive. Stalin wanted to have Ryutin executed but Sergei Mironovich Kirov, Stalin's Politburo protégé, opposed such a move, so Ryutin was initially sentenced to ten years' imprisonment. However, he was re-arrested in 1936 on a trumped-up charge of terrorism. Under torture, he refused to recant or admit any of the false accusations that had been made against him. Nevertheless, he was executed on 10 January 1937.

The Kirov Affair

By then, Stalin had already begun a purge to remove all those who might be opposed to him. The Politburo, ostensibly an elected body, was hand-picked by Stalin, who became the sole fount of Communist ideology. In 1933 alone, 400,000 people were expelled from the Communist Party. But the Great Purge began in earnest after the assassination of Sergey Kirov.

Born in 1886, Kirov had become a Bolshevik after the 1905 Revolution. He fought in the Russian Civil War and became head of the Party in Azerbaijan. After the death of Lenin he wisely became a supporter of Stalin and went on to

Pictured together like master and pupil, Stalin with Sergey Kirov. When the pupil dared to stray, the master had him shot like a dog

become head of the Party in Leningrad. Kirov became extraordinarily popular in the Party, but Stalin saw him as a threat after his opposition to the execution of Ryutin, so he offered him a position in Moscow, where he thought he could rein him in. However, Kirov remained in Leningrad. On 1 December 1934, Kirov was shot and killed outside his office in the Smolny Institute by deranged Party official Leonid Nikolaev. It is thought that the assassination was arranged by Yagoda on the orders of Stalin. Nikolaev was tried in secret and then shot and his wife was also executed. His son was sent to an orphanage, while the other members of his family were liquidated or sent to the Gulag.

There was only one witness to the assassination and that was Kirov's unarmed bodyguard, Commissar Borisov, who died on the day after the murder when he fell from the back of an NKVD truck. His wife was confined to a lunatic asylum. The man who had provided Nikolaev with the murder weapon was also shot.

Stalin rushed to Leningrad in order to 'investigate' the murder, but the real reason for his visit was to turn attention away from the NKVD. He helped carry the coffin at Kirov's funeral and ensured that cities were named after him and statues were erected in his honour. It was subsequently announced that Stalin had personally interrogated the assassin and that 'the leaders of the Opposition placed the gun in Nikolaev's hand'.

According to a Communist Party communiqué, the killing of Kirov was a 'fascist plot' that had been orchestrated by an unidentified foreign diplomat. Some 104 defendants, who were already in prison at the time of the assassination, were also convicted of complicity and executed. Kamenev and Zinoviev were also arrested and charged with 'moral complicity' in the assassination. Kamenev was sentenced to five years' imprisonment and Zinoviev to ten.

Kirov's assassination became the excuse for the Great Purge of 1936–8. At that time the Soviet Union was under threat from Germany and an expansionist Japan.

THE KIROV DECREE

On his way to Leningrad to investigate Kirov's murder, Stalin drafted a decree. It was published the following day and it read,

'The case of those accused of preparing or committing terrorist acts is to be dealt with in an accelerated way, judicial organs may not hold up the carrying out of death sentences because of appeals for mercy from criminals of this category. The organs of the NKVD are to carry out death sentences passed on criminals of the above categories as soon as the court has pronounced sentence.'

In order to speed up the process further, he later added,

1. *The investigation of such cases must be completed in no more than ten days.*
2. *The charges will be handed to the accused 24 hours before the court examines the case.*
3. *The case will be heard with no participation by other parties [that is, no witnesses were to be called].*
4. *No appeals for quashing the verdict or for mercy will be allowed.*
5. *The death sentence is to be carried out as soon as it has been pronounced.*

The decree was approved by the Politburo on 4 December 1934. On the following day, dozens of people who had not been charged in connection with the Kirov assassination were executed by the NKVD and before the month was over almost a hundred others were eliminated in the same way.

The Soviet press saw fascist spies everywhere. Hundreds of people were rounded up and herded into police vans or inconspicuous vehicles, so that the victims would not be warned of their arrest in advance and the general public would not be alerted. They were taken to the headquarters of the State Security Division of the NKVD in Lubyanka Square, the most feared building in Moscow. There they were kept in windowless cells under electric lights that burned day and night.

The Moscow Show Trials

There were to be show trials that would 'put an end once and for all to the foul subversive work against the foundations of the Soviet state', Stalin said. Kamenev, Zinoviev and 14 other defendants would appear at the first of these. The group had already been blamed for the assassination of Kirov. They were then charged with having joined with Trotsky in order to form a terrorist organization that would remove Stalin from power and then execute him. At first, Kamenev and Zinoviev refused to confess, so Yagoda was put in charge of their interrogation. His techniques included repeated beatings, torture, making prisoners stand or go without sleep for days on end, and threats to arrest and execute the prisoners' families – for instance, Kamenev's teenage son was arrested and charged with terrorism.

After months of such interrogation, the defendants were driven to despair and exhaustion. Eventually, they agreed to confess if the Politburo promised to spare their lives, along with those of their families and friends. However, when they appeared before the Politburo only Stalin, defence minister Kliment Voroshilov and Yagoda's deputy Nikolai Yezhov were present. Stalin first explained that this three-man commission had been appointed by the Politburo and then he gave them the promised assurances. The 'Trial of the Sixteen' took place publicly before the Military Collegium of the Supreme Court of the USSR at the October Hall of the House of the Unions in Moscow on 19–24 August 1934. The defendants were flanked by armed guards with fixed bayonets.

The procurator general and chief prosecutor Andrey Vyshinksy read out the four articles of the indictment, from which the following is an excerpt.

> 'During the period from 1932 to 1936 a joint Trotskyist-Zinovievist Centre was organized in Moscow which set itself the task of carrying out a number of acts of terror against the leaders of the Communist Party of the Soviet Union (Bolsheviks) in order to arrogate power to itself... That one of these terrorist groups, which was operating under the direct instructions of Zinoviev and Trotsky as well as those of the Joint Trotskyist Centre... perpetrated the despicable murder of Comrade S. M. Kirov...'

According to Vyshinsky, left-wing Bolsheviks such as Trotsky had allied themselves

Now you see them, now you don't: top, Lenin addresses the crowd in 1920, with Kamenev and Trotsky in attendance; above, Lenin's comrades have completely disappeared thanks to Stalin's retouching artists

with the Nazis who had come to power in Germany, in order to impose a fascist dictatorship on Russia. Western journalists who were allowed to attend the trial found this incredible. However, all of the accused confessed openly in court.

'All defendants seemed eager to heap accusation upon accusation upon themselves,' wrote one observer. 'They required little cross-examination by the prosecutor.' Kamenev even said, 'No matter what the sentence may be, I consider it just.' Vyshinsky then addressed the court.

> *'Shoot these rabid dogs. Death to this gang who hide their ferocious teeth, their eagle claws, from the people! Down with that vulture Trotsky, from whose mouth a bloody venom drips, putrefying the great ideals of Marxism!... Down with these abject animals! Let's put an end once and for all to these miserable hybrids of foxes and pigs, these stinking corpses! Let's exterminate the mad dogs of capitalism, who want to tear to pieces the flower of our new Soviet nation! Let's push the bestial hatred they bear our leaders back down their own throats!'*

When they were all found guilty, one of the accused shouted, 'Long live the cause of Marx, Engels, Lenin and Stalin.'

Despite the assurances they had received from Stalin, the accused were

A. Y. Vyshinsky [above] wrote, 'Criminal law is a tool of the class struggle.' In the Moscow show trials, verdicts were predetermined, with evidence obtained through torture and threats to serve Stalin's lust for power

sentenced to death and shot in the back of the head soon afterwards. Most of their relatives were also arrested and shot.

ANDREY YANUARYEVICH VYSHINSKY (1883–1954)

Born to a noble family of Polish Catholics in Odessa, Vyshinsky became a Menshevik in 1903. In accordance with the decision of the Provisional Government, he even signed an order to arrest Lenin. But in 1920 he joined the Bolsheviks and in 1933 he organized a systemic drive against 'harvest-wreckers and grain-thieves' after the harvest had failed to match central estimates. He came to international prominence as a prosecutor in the 1933 Metro-Vickers trial, where six British and twelve Soviet engineers were convicted of wrecking power stations and spying for British intelligence. At the 'Trial of the Sixteen', he condemned the accused as 'liars and clowns, miserable pygmies, lapdogs and yappers' and demanded the death penalty. In his closing statement to the court, he said,

'I now conclude, comrades judges. The last hour is approaching, the hour of reckoning for these people who have committed grave crimes against our great country. It is the last hour of reckoning for these people who took up arms against our dearest and most beloved, against the beloved leaders of our Party and our country, against Stalin…

'I want to conclude by reminding you, comrades judges, of those demands which the law makes in cases of the gravest crimes against the state. I take the liberty of reminding you that it is your duty, once you find these people, all sixteen of them, guilty of crimes against the state, to apply to them in full measure those articles of the law which have been pre- ferred against them by the prosecution.

'I demand that dogs gone mad should be shot – every one of them!'

In 1947, Vyshinsky justified his new departures in jurisprudence in a monograph entitled *Theory of Judicial Proofs in Soviet Justice*. In it, he said, 'Criminal law is a tool of the class struggle.' That a defendant admitted their crime was enough, because 'confession of the accused is the queen of evidence'. Not above helping himself, Vyshinsky misappropriated the money and the house of one of the defendants during the Moscow trials.

He headed the government of Latvia after it was annexed by the Soviet Union in 1940 and he arranged for a Communist government to take over in Romania in 1945. When King Michael protested that the country's independence was guaranteed by the Yalta Agreement, Vyshinsky answered, 'I am Yalta.'

He died in New York while serving as the representative of the Soviet Union at the United Nations and is buried near Red Square.

The 'Trial of the Seventeen' followed in January 1937. Again the defendants were leading Communists who were accused of plotting treason against the Soviet government in collusion with Trotsky. All were found guilty. Thirteen were executed and the other four were imprisoned in the Gulag. One of them was Karl Radek, who had travelled back to Russia on the 'sealed train' with Lenin. His life was spared so that he could provide – or be forced to provide – evidence against others in subsequent trials. Later he was reportedly killed in the camps by another

Karl Radek was an international Communist who travelled in the 'sealed train' with Lenin, but he made the mistake of making jokes about Stalin

inmate. However, it was discovered that he had been killed by an NKVD agent on the direct orders of Lavrenty Beria. Radek and the other defendants were exonerated in 1988. It is thought that Stalin ordered Beria to have Radek killed because Radek told a number of jokes about him.

Yet Stalin appeared to have a sense of humour – as long as the joke was not on him. In 2009, a series of 19 pictures that offered an insight into Stalin's mind went on show in Moscow. They were all male nudes and they had been sketched by a number of 19th-century Russian painters. The interesting thing is that Stalin had defaced them all. In one picture he had scribbled out the genital area with red pencil and in another he had drawn a large blue cross across the man's torso, but in most of the portraits he had restricted himself to captions in the bottom corner, some of them signed. Next to one picture of a pensive nude, Stalin had written, 'One thinking fool is worse than 10 enemies.'

Others had messages for Bolshevik comrades, both dead and alive. Alongside a muscular male nude drawn from the back by Vasily Surikov, Stalin had written, 'Radek, you ginger bastard, if you hadn't pissed into the wind, if you hadn't been

NIKOLAI IVANOVICH YEZHOV (1895–1939)

Nicknamed 'the Dwarf' because of his diminutive stature – he was little more than five feet tall – Yezhov was also lame. Yet he was responsible for the worst period of the Great Purge, which is sometimes known as the *Yezhovshchina* (the 'Yezhov era' or the 'Hedgehog era'), since *Yezh* means 'hedgehog'.

Yezhov joined the Bolsheviks in March 1917. He was a political commissar during the Russian Civil War and he rose to become one of Stalin's favourites. By April 1933, he was a member of the newly formed Purge Commission that ejected more than a million members from the Party. In the following year he became a full member of the Central Committee and he succeeded Lazar Kaganovich as chairman of the Party Control Commission. With little more than an elementary education, he prepared the papers outlining the ideological basis of the Moscow show trials.

At Stalin's behest, he succeeded Yagoda as head of the NKVD in 1936. His first task was to investigate and execute Yagoda, which he did with remorseless zeal. After that he was given a free hand to fulfil arbitrary quotas of arrests and executions. He maintained that it was better to make 'ten innocent people suffer than let one "enemy of the people" escape'. Under Yezhov, the number of NKVD agents and torturers quadrupled. Their methods were based on a study of Hitler's Gestapo. Making an anti-Stalin joke in a bar was only one of the countless offences that could lead to imprisonment or death. The cellars under the Lubyanka could no longer handle the numbers Yezhov executed, so an abattoir was constructed in an adjacent courtyard. Its rear wall was made from logs, which absorbed the bullets, and there were hoses to wash away the blood.

At a gala held at the Bolshoi Theatre on 20 December 1937, banners portraying Yezhov hung beside those of Stalin. Stalin's trade minister Anastas Mikoyan praised Yezhov to the gathering. 'Learn the Stalin way to work from Comrade Yezhov, just as he learned and will continue to learn from Comrade Stalin himself.'

Mikoyan's words were greeted by thunderous applause, but it was the beginning of the end for Yezhov. Stalin did not like rivals. On 22 August 1938, Stalin appointed fellow Georgian Lavrenty Beria as Yezhov's deputy. Sensing his fate, Yezhov began drinking heavily. Soon afterwards, he was relieved of his post and Beria took over his duties. After being arrested on 10 April 1939, he confessed to several capital crimes and gross sexual deviancy – which might well have been the case. When he was tried in Beria's office he fell to his knees and begged for a brief audience with Stalin, so that he could explain himself. He vowed to die with Stalin's name on his lips. After being sentenced to death, he was stripped naked and beaten on Beria's orders. It was poetic justice, for Yezhov had ordered Yagoda's final humiliation in just the same way. Dragged to the execution yard in a state of semi-collapse, Yezhov wept uncontrollably as he was shot.

so bad, you'd still be alive.'

On another sketch of a bearded nude man, Stalin had drawn a red inverted triangle over the man's penis and written, 'Why are you so thin?'

This is thought to have been aimed at Mikhail Ivanovich Kalinin, who was titular head of the Soviet state from 1919 until his death in 1946. Kalinin was one of the few survivors of the Great Purge, though Stalin still marginalized him. However, his wife was arrested in 1938 and tortured into confessing to 'counter-revolutionary Trotskyite activities'. She was sent to a labour camp and only released in 1945, shortly before her husband's death.

Some of the captions show a crude, sexualized sense of humour. Although another man is pictured naked from the back, his hand appears to reach down to his genitals. In the bottom corner, in red pencil, Stalin had scrawled, 'You need to work, not wank. Time for re-education.' Another shows a naked man standing over a prostrate naked woman. Stalin has captioned this one, 'Idiot!!! You've completely forgotten what to do.'

Nikolai Yezhov was nicknamed 'the Dwarf' and nothing gave him more pleasure than executing innocent victims

Most of the captions are in Russian, though some are in Stalin's native Georgian. They are thought to have been written at some point between 1939 and 1946. It is unclear whether Stalin intended to share his 'humour' with others or just keep it to himself.

The Red Army had been purged repeatedly of tsarist officers and those sympathetic to Trotsky, following his removal as commissar of war. But in 1937 Radek had provided evidence against Marshal Mikhail Tukhachevsky, who was arrested along with seven other Red Army commanders. They were charged with organizing a Trotskyite, anti-Soviet conspiracy and spying for Germany. The evidence needed to be reasonably convincing, so the NKVD came up with an elaborate plan. They fed Reinhard Heydrich, head of the intelligence service of the Nazi SS, with the story that Tukhachevsky had hatched a plot against Stalin. Heydrich improved on this information by providing a series of forged documents that purported to show

Nikolai Krestinsky [wearing hat] is pictured in a retouched photograph of a 1920 Central Committee meeting. Leonid Serebryakov is to Lenin's right

that Tukhachevsky was working for Germany, but Stalin decided not to use them. Instead the defendants were tortured into making bogus confessions. They were tried in secret and executed on the night of 11 June 1937 – Stalin had ordered that they were to be shot directly after their court martials. All were exonerated in 1957.

The executions of the army commanders were swiftly followed by the arrest of most of the people's commissars, nearly all of the regional Party secretaries, hundreds of Central Committee members and candidates and thousands of lesser Communist Party officials. In the Red Army, three out of the five Soviet marshals, 90 per cent of the generals, 80 per cent of the colonels and 30,000 officers of lesser rank were purged. In all, 37,761 officers and commissars were dismissed from the army, 10,868 were arrested and 7,211 were condemned for anti-Soviet crimes. Virtually all of them were executed.

The third show trial was the 'Trial of the Twenty-One' in March 1938. The leading defendants were Nikolai Bukharin and Aleksey Rykov. Among other things they were accused of killing Kirov and Menzhinsky; poisoning novelist Maxim Gorky and his son; plotting to assassinate Lenin and Stalin; wrecking the economy by sabotaging mines, derailing trains, killing cattle and putting nails and glass into butter; undermining the country's military power; spying for the Germans, French, Japanese and British; and making secret agreements to surrender territory in the west and the far east of Russia to foreign powers. Some of these charges were plainly absurd and some of the defendants refused to confess, so Stalin intervened personally. Until that point Yagoda had been the defendants' interrogator, but Stalin replaced him with Nikolai Yezhov. Yagoda then became one of the defendants. Also on trial were two of the doctors who had refused to sign the falsified death certificate after the death of Stalin's wife.

On the first day of the trial Nikolai Krestinsky, a former member of the Politburo and Soviet ambassador to Germany, declared his innocence to the presiding judge Vasili Ulrikh.

> 'I do not recognize that I am guilty. I am not a Trotskyite. I was never a member of the right-winger and Trotskyite bloc, which I did not know existed. Nor have I committed a single one of the crimes imputed to me personally and in particular I am not guilty of having maintained relations with the German intelligence service.'

He returned to court on the following day with a dislocated shoulder. This time his plea had totally changed.

> 'Yesterday, under the influence of a momentary keen feeling of false shame, evoked by the atmosphere of the dock and the painful impression created by the public reading of the indictment, which was aggravated by my poor health, I could not bring myself to tell the truth. I could not bring myself to say that I was guilty. And instead of saying, "Yes, I am guilty," I almost mechanically answered, "No, I am not guilty"'

Bukharin held out for three months, but brutal treatment and threats to his young wife and son wore him down and he finally made a confession. However, he changed his mind when it was amended and corrected by Stalin. After being brutally cross-examined he ended up by confessing only his general culpability, without admitting any specific charges.

With his hands handcuffed behind his back and his trousers falling down, Yagoda admitted poisoning his predecessor Menzhinsky and attempting to poison his successor Yezhov with mercury vapour. He declared that he sympathized with Bukharin and he also 'admitted' working for the German, Japanese and Polish intelligence services. Desperately pleading for his life, he begged to be allowed to work as a labourer.

All of the defendants were found guilty and all but three were shot. On Yezhov's orders Yagoda was first of all stripped naked and beaten, as an extra humiliation. Two years later, Yezhov would suffer the same fate on the instructions of Beria. Some witnesses claimed that Bukharin and Rykov faced their executioners cursing Stalin, but according to another account Bukharin was so utterly destroyed by his treatment that he was still swearing allegiance to his leader when he died. His wife Anna Larina was separated from their one-year-old child and sent to the Gulag, along with the wives of the other defendants. Yagoda's wife was sentenced to eight years' imprisonment, but was executed a year later. The three defendants that were spared were sentenced to long terms in the Gulag before being summarily executed in September 1941.

Many Western observers who attended the Moscow trials reported that they were fair. After all, the defendants had apparently freely confessed in open court and there was no evidence that they had been tortured or drugged. United States ambassador Joseph E. Davies appeared to be convinced of their guilt. As he wrote in *Mission to Moscow* in 1942,

> *'In view of the character of the accused, their long terms of service, their recognized distinction in their profession, their long-continued loyalty to the Communist cause, it is scarcely credible that their brother officers... should have acquiesced in their execution, unless they were convinced that these men had been guilty of some offense. It is generally accepted by members of the Diplomatic Corps that the accused must have been guilty of an offense which in the Soviet Union would merit the death penalty.'*

Davies sat through the Bukharin trial six months later and heard 'evidence which, if true, more than justified this action. Undoubtedly those facts were all fully known to the military court at this time'.

Communist sympathizers in Western countries echoed these views and they denounced criticism of the trials as capitalist attempts to subvert communism. As the British Labour Party MP Denis Pritt wrote,

> *'Once again the more faint-hearted socialists are beset with doubts and anxieties [but] once again we can feel confident that when the smoke has rolled away from the battlefield of controversy it will be realized that the charge was true, the confessions correct and the prosecution fairly conducted.'*

Pritt was expelled from the Labour Party in 1940 for supporting the Soviet invasion of Finland, though he was awarded the International Stalin Peace Prize in 1954.

The general secretary of the Communist Party of Great Britain, Harry Pollitt, wrote in the *Daily Worker* of 12 March 1936 that 'the trials in Moscow represent a new triumph in the history of progress'. Ironically, the article was illustrated by a photograph of Stalin with Nikolai Yezhov, who would soon be executed. Afterwards, he was airbrushed from official photographs by NKVD archivists.

In the United States, left-wing playwright Lillian Hellman and others also denounced criticism of the trials. But not everyone was so gullible. It was the end of the road for some prominent former Communists such as Bertram Wolfe, Jay Lovestone and Arthur Koestler, who then became fervent anti-Communists.

NKVD ORDER NUMBER 00447

On 30 July 1937, NKVD Order Number 00447 was passed to speed up the 'repression of former *kulaks*, criminals and other anti-Soviet elements'. Ordered by Stalin, it was signed by Nikolai Yezhov. NKVD 'troikas' (commissions of three people) were set up at all levels across the Soviet Union. They replaced centralized six-man 'Special Boards', which included the Prosecutor-General or his deputy as well as senior members of the NKVD. The troika, by contrast, consisted of the local NKVD chief, the provincial first secretary and the chairman of the local executive committee or a representative of the prosecutor's office, though sometimes only two of them were present.

Like the Special Boards the troikas handed down judgements, condemning the accused to death or long periods in the Gulag. The defendants did not even appear, but were simply handed the written judgements in their cells. While the paperwork was all-important, executions under this system were carried out in secret. It was usual for the NKVD chief to initial the sentence in the first instance, with the other two adding their initials after it had been carried out.

In Uzbekistan, the appointed troika ordered the execution of 40,000 people in 1937 and 1938, while one million individuals perished across the entire Soviet Union under the same system. This was over and above those sentenced to death by authorities such as the supreme courts of the Soviet Union and its autonomous republics and military tribunals. Other executions were carried out by 'special order'. There was not even the pretence of a trial.

Orders for more killings came directly from Moscow. Yezhov sent a telegram to the NKVD chief in Frunze, the capital of Kirgizia, ordering him to execute 10,000 'enemies of the people'. With the reply came a numbered list of those who had been shot. An order for another 15,000 executions then went out to Sverdlovsk. In February 1938 Yezhov called a special NKVD conference in Kiev, where he ordered another 30,000 executions in Ukraine.

The troika system was dropped with the fall of Yezhov, though Special Board trials continued through Stalin's reign. However the troikas were reintroduced when Poland, Latvia, Finland and Romania were purged after they were occupied.

As the purge continued, Stalin put all of the surviving members of the Lenin-era Politburo on trial. Almost every important Bolshevik from the Revolution was executed. Of 1,966 delegates to the Party congress in 1934, 1,108 were arrested, including 98 of the 139 members of the Central Committee. Stalin even ordered the execution of Leon Trotsky, who was living in exile abroad. Trotsky was assassinated by a Soviet agent in Mexico in 1940. Outside politics and the Red Army, literally millions of ordinary people also died in the purges, but most of their tragic stories have been lost to history.

CHAPTER NINE

THE GREAT PATRIOTIC WAR

In August 1939 the Soviet Union entered into a non-aggression treaty with Germany. Stalin's purges had left the Red Army too weak to stand up to Germany, so the pact represented a measure of security for the Soviet Union. At the same time Germany's eastern border would be protected. The partition of Poland began with Germany's invasion on 1 September 1939. Two days later, Britain and France declared war on Germany. In spite of the pact, Hitler attacked the Soviet Union in June 1941, forcing Stalin to defend his homeland in what became known to Russians as the 'Great Patriotic War'.

Stalingrad was the graveyard for Nazi hopes of conquering the world. Fought between July 1942 and February 1943, it was one of the bloodiest battles ever, ending with 2 million casualties and defeat for Hitler's 6th Army

IDEOLOGICALLY, **S**TALIN AND **H**ITLER SHOULD HAVE BEEN ENEMIES. Stalin was a left-wing Communist who espoused the power of the people and the concept of internationalism while Hitler was a right-wing demagogue who believed in the racial superiority of the German people. Hitler condemned the Bolsheviks as Jews and the two men even supported opposite sides in the Spanish Civil War. However, they had much in common. Stalin's NKVD imitated the tactics of Hitler's secret police, the Gestapo, and Stalin's purges emulated Hitler's 'Night of the Long Knives', when in June 1934 Ernst Röhm and dozens of other Nazi leaders were summarily executed in order to consolidate Hitler's power.

While Stalin admired Hitler and his methods, Germany's leader was an implacable enemy of Communism. In his book *Mein Kampf*, Hitler regarded the east as nothing more than a source of *Lebensraum* (living space) for the German people. He saw the Slavs who lived there as subhuman, fit only to provide slave labour for his Reich. Meanwhile, further to the east was the expansionist Japan, who had fought and beaten the Russians in the Russo-Japanese War of 1904–5 and had made more recent incursions into Siberia.

THE SPANISH CIVIL WAR (1936–9)

In 1936, the Spanish army under General Francisco Franco [*right*] rebelled against the left-wing Republican government. In the ensuing conflict, Hitler and the Italian dictator Benito Mussolini backed Franco's Nationalist force and the German *Luftwaffe* carried out the first carpet bombing of the Basque market town of Guernica in 1937.

Taking the opposite stance, the Soviet Union supported the besieged Republican government. However, the Communist International Brigades – which were made up of volunteers from Europe and the United States – were split between the followers of Stalin and Trotsky. This made Stalin uneasy, so the NKVD sent along agent Alexander Orlov, who fabricated evidence that led to the arrest and purge of the leaders of the Workers' Party of Marxist Unification (POUM). He was also responsible for the kidnapping and disappearance of other anti-Stalinist Communists who were fighting for the Republicans, including Trotsky's former secretary Erwin Wolf and Mark Rein, son of a Menshevik leader.

Orlov also organized the transport of 510 tons of gold from the Spanish treasury. The Spaniards thought they were buying Soviet military supplies, but once the bullion was safely in Moscow Stalin threw a party.

'The Spaniards will never see their gold again, just as one cannot see one's own ears,' he announced jubilantly.

Orlov was awarded the Order of Lenin, though he later defected. Thanks partially to Orlov and Stalin, the Republicans lost the Spanish Civil War and Franco remained as the Fascist dictator of Spain until 1975.

Stalin's Deportations

However, while the Soviet Union faced these external threats, Stalin tackled what he saw as more pressing problems within its borders. In the event of war, Stalin believed that he could not depend on the loyalty of the Volga Germans, the Muslims in the southern states, the Crimean Tartars or the six other nationalities who had opposed the imposition of Soviet power in the 1920s and 1930s. They might easily be induced to side with the Germans. As a result, some one and a half million people were uprooted and resettled in remote areas where they would pose no threat.

The deportations were organized by Lavrenty Beria. They began with show trials of local leaders and then sentences of execution, imprisonment or deportation would be handed out by the NKVD troikas. Stalin and Molotov signed the authorization to remove over 172,000 Koreans from the border regions of the Soviet Far East in order to prevent 'Japanese espionage'. Ukraine was depopulated once again. This time the Poles who had farmed there for generations were sent eastwards.

One summer's evening in 1936, the Polish and German men who lived in the village of Zytomierz were summoned to the local council and told that 'for their own good' they and their families were being sent away. They were not told where. The doors were locked and the men were held in custody for a week while their families packed their belongings and sold their livestock. They were then jammed into cattle trucks and sent on a two-week rail journey to Kazakhstan, where they were dumped in a desolate spot on the steppe. Marked by a sign that said 'Village Number 2', it had a newly dug well. Officials taught them to make bricks from mud and straw and showed them how to burn animal dung for fuel. They were lucky. Other deportees were dumped on to the steppe with no instructions or tools, so

THE VOLGA GERMANS

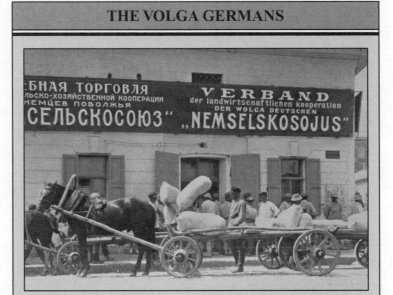

When Catherine the Great displaced her husband Peter III and took the Russian throne in 1762, she opened Russia's borders to European settlers. Catherine was German by birth so she encouraged a large number of Germans to settle along the Volga, where they maintained their German culture. In 1924, a Volga German Autonomous Soviet Socialist Republic was established. It was dissolved by Stalin when Germany invaded the Soviet Union and on 8 August 1941 he signed a Decree of Banishment. Even though the Volga Germans no longer spoke German, and had long lost any connection with their homeland, they were still committed Lutherans and as such they opposed the irreligious Bolsheviks. Some 400,000 ethnic Germans were stripped of their land and houses and were deported eastwards to Kazakhstan in Soviet Central Asia, Altai Krai in Siberia and other far-flung places. They were given just four hours to pack and then they were frogmarched to the rail embarkation points. One hundred and fifty-one convoys embarked from 19 stations. Those who attempted to stay behind in their homes were dragged out and shot. During the war the deportees were used as slave labour, but around a third did not survive the rigours of the camps.

they could only fashion very crude homes dug from the earth. Many died in their first winter there.

The Molotov-Ribbentrop Pact

In 1936, Germany and Japan signed an Anti-Comintern Pact. The two nations were later joined by Italy. This agreement posed a genuine threat to the Soviet Union, which made it the natural ally of Britain and France, who were opposing German expansionism in the west. All three countries then signed a treaty with Czechoslovakia. However, Hitler continued to make inflammatory speeches in which he demanded that the Germans in the Sudetenland, which was part of Czechoslovakia, were returned to the fatherland. Anxious to avoid military conflict, Britain and France attended a peace conference at Munich in September 1938. In view of Hitler's strident anti-Soviet rhetoric, they decided that the Soviet Union's participation would not assist their cause. Besides, the Soviet Union was thought to be of little use as an ally, because the Red Army had been weakened by Stalin's purges. In the Munich Agreement that followed, the Sudetenland was returned to Germany, which went on to swallow up the rest of Czechoslovakia in March 1939.

It seemed to Stalin that Hitler might now be tempted to demand territory from the Soviet Union. As Britain and France had done nothing to defend Czechoslovakia, it seemed unlikely that they would go to war to aid the Soviet Union, so there was no point in making an alliance with them. What is more, Britain and France might actively encourage a war between Nazi Germany and Soviet Russia in the hope that it would destroy them both. Meanwhile, Germany and the Soviet Union were already in talks. Facing a possible blockade by Britain, Germany would need raw materials from the Soviet Union in any coming war, while the Russians needed German technology and know-how to help them industrialize.

Britain and France then offered a guarantee to Poland, but Stalin had little time for the Polish army and he could hardly expect it to maintain a buffer state between an aggressive Germany and the Soviet motherland. In May 1939, Stalin replaced his foreign minister Maxim Litvinov with Molotov, who began negotiations with German foreign minister Joachim von Ribbentrop. They signed a non-aggression pact – known colloquially as the Molotov-Ribbentrop Pact – in the presence of Stalin in Moscow on 23 August. The pact contained a secret protocol which allowed the Soviet Union to occupy Finland, Estonia and Latvia. Lithuania, which bordered the German province of East Prussia, would be German. The secret protocol also called for the division of Poland.

It is conceivable that if Stalin had maintained his alliance with Britain and France, Hitler might have thought twice about invading Poland and the Second World War – which resulted in up to 60 million deaths and caused untold misery – might not have happened. As it was, Hitler had a free hand. On 1 September 1939,

VYACHESLAV MIKHAYLOVICH MOLOTOV (1890–1986)

Born Vyacheslav Mikhaylovich Skryabin, Molotov [*seen right with Stalin at the Kremlin*] joined the Bolshevik faction of the Russian Social-Democratic Workers' Party in 1906 and adopted the pseudonym 'Molotov' for his revolutionary activities. Arrested in 1909 and 1913, he spent four years in exile. During the Russian Civil War he was sent to Ukraine, though he took no part in the fighting. An early supporter of Stalin, he became a member of the Central Committee in 1921 and the Politburo in 1926. He replaced Aleksey Rykov as chairman of the Council of People's Commissars – i.e. prime minister – in December 1930, a post he held until 1941.

In May 1939, Stalin appointed Molotov people's commissar of foreign affairs. Molotov then negotiated a non-aggression pact with Hitler's foreign minister Joachim von Ribbentrop. Stalin took over as prime minister in May 1941, with Molotov as his deputy. After Germany attacked the Soviet Union in June 1941, Molotov became a member of the war cabinet and he arranged the Soviet alliance with Great Britain and the United States. His name became so closely linked with war that the Finns applied the term 'Molotov cocktail' to an incendiary device that was made from a bottle of flammable liquids. It was used against the Russians in 1939–40 and 1941–4, and against the Germans in 1944–5.

Molotov attended the Allied summits at Tehran in 1943 and Yalta and Potsdam in 1945. He also attended the San Francisco Conference in 1945, at which the United

Nations was created. Although his wife was sent to the Gulag in 1948, he remained foreign minister until 1949, a post he resumed after the death of Stalin in 1953. However, his close identification with the Stalin regime caused friction with the anti-Stalin Nikita Khrushchev and he was dismissed in 1956. He tried unsuccessfully to have Khrushchev deposed, but he was despatched as Soviet ambassador to Mongolia and then became a delegate to the International Atomic Energy Agency in Vienna. After more disagreements with Khrushchev he was expelled from the Communist Party in 1962 and he retired to private life.

Germany invaded western Poland and two days later Britain and France declared war on Germany. But there was little they could do to help the Polish because on 17 September the Red Army occupied eastern Poland. The Soviet Union was expelled from the League of Nations, but no one declared war.

The Red Army captured a large number of Polish prisoners of war. The officers were separated and along with members of the intelligentsia they were taken to the Katyn Forest, west of Smolensk, and murdered. According to some estimates up to 22,000 prisoners were massacred between April and May 1940. Recent evidence shows that Stalin personally signed the order for the Katyn massacre. At a single stroke, Stalin had removed the whole of a nation's elite and with it any effective opposition to Soviet rule. All of the inhabitants of eastern Poland were now citizens of the Soviet empire. In 1940 and 1941 as many as one and a half million people were deported, mostly to Siberia and Kazakhstan.

By the summer of 1940 the Soviet Union occupied the Baltic states. The NKVD was sent in to remove any opposition and their orders were brutally specific.

'Operations shall begin at daybreak. Upon entering the home of the person to be deported, the senior member of the operative group shall assemble the entire family of the deportee into one room... In view of the fact that a large number of deportees must be arrested and distributed in special camps and that their families must proceed to special settlements in regions, it is essential that the operations of removal of both the members of the deportee's family and its head shall be carried out simultaneously without notifying them of the separation confronting them.'

Deportees were transported in cattle trucks with a hole cut in the floor to serve as a lavatory. They were fed thin soup, bread and salt fish. Many died from dehydration, especially infants and the elderly. Any attempt to escape by ripping out the floors proved fatal because the guards had fitted steel scythes under the last carriage.

Soviet troops on the outskirts of Warsaw in 1944: although styled the army of liberation, they were about to enslave Poland once more

Anyone dropping down on to the track would be cut in half.

With Russia supplying the raw materials he needed, Hitler could attack in the west. Germany quickly invaded Norway, Belgium, Holland and France. However, in the Battle of Britain, the *Luftwaffe* failed to establish air superiority over Britain, making an invasion impossible. Nevertheless, on 22 June 1941 Hitler tore up the Molotov-Ribbentrop Pact and attacked Russia. Stalin was so shocked that he went into a state of nervous collapse and did not speak to anyone for 11 days.

Repelling the Invader

But Stalin refused to let the Red Army make a

Pravda on 23 June 1941, the day after Germany attacked the Soviet Union. Stalin looks commanding above, but he nearly had a breakdown

strategic withdrawal. When Hitler's Panzer spearheads reached Minsk on 29 June 1941 they encircled four Soviet armies, taking 287,000 prisoners. On 16 July, the German pincers surrounded Smolensk taking a further 300,000 Russian soldiers captive and by 26 September Kiev had yielded up a further 665,000 captives. By October the Germans were menacing Leningrad. Another 663,000 hostages were taken at Vyazma and 100,000 more surrendered at Bryansk. Stalin had not signed the Geneva Convention, so Soviet prisoners of war had no protection. They were frequently maltreated and starved to death by their German guards, who regarded them as less than human. Those who survived German captivity were despatched to the Gulag when they returned.

With the collapse of the Red Army, the road to Moscow was now open.

A triumphant Marshal Zhukov at the Reichstag in 1945. In 1941, he had been recalled to defend Moscow. It is thought that Stalin then retired to his dacha on the edge of Moscow where he had a bunker in case of enemy attack

Diplomats were evacuated and the embalmed body of Lenin was removed from his tomb on Red Square for safekeeping. Stalin was about to flee the city. A train was prepared but at the last moment he decided to stay and fight the invader. He recalled his ablest general, Georgy Konstantinovich Zhukov, to command the defence of Moscow. The Germans were within 20 miles of the city when their advance stalled.

They found themselves confronted by Russia's greatest general – General Winter. The winter of 1941 was the coldest for 140 years, but Hitler had been so confident of a quick victory that the German soldiers had not been provided with winter clothing.

To the north the German army besieged Leningrad and to the south it reached Stalingrad. Refusing to give up the city that bore his name, Stalin sent millions of ill-trained, often unarmed men into the fray – they were told to pick up the rifle of the man in front of them when he was killed. General Zhukov was then sent to

THE SECOND WORLD WAR

Stalin insisted that the Red Army was fighting the Great Patriotic War to defend the motherland but the Soviet contribution to the wider European war can hardly be underestimated. Between June 1941 and July 1943, the Soviet Union faced the German army alone on the Continent, while Britain and America were confined

to fighting in North Africa and pursuing an air offensive against Germany's cities. But while the British and the Americans were risking their lives to supply the Russians by manning Arctic convoys to Archangel and Murmansk, Stalin [*seen in a patriotic Soviet postcard above*] demanded the Western Allies open a second front.

The Anglo-American landings in Sicily and Italy in the summer of 1943, and a planned invasion of Greece, threatened to cut the Red Army off from Germany – its prize. So Stalin urged the Western Allies to land in France, which they did in June 1944. Both sides then raced for Berlin. However, early in 1945 the Supreme Allied Commander General, Dwight D. Eisenhower, diverted the American forces to the south to prevent the German army establishing a redoubt in Bavaria, which allowed the Red Army to take Berlin.

The Soviet Union took no part in the fighting in the Far East. After a brief border war in Manchuria in 1939, Stalin signed a non-aggression pact with Japan in 1941. He continued to observe the non-aggression pact even though Japan was allied with Germany, who had attacked the Soviet Union. Although the Soviet Union allied itself to Britain in June 1941, and to the United States after the Japanese attack on Pearl Harbor that December, Stalin refused to break the treaty. The Soviet Union did not declare war on Japan until 8 August 1945, two days after the first atomic bomb had been dropped on Hiroshima. By the time Japan surrendered a week later, the Red Army had taken more than 2.7 million prisoners. Only a few hundred thousand ever returned.

Some eight million Soviet troops died in the Second World War, while the Americans got off comparatively lightly with 298,131 deaths. Britain lost 357,116, including 92,673 civilians, while there were 277,077 military casualties. The British Commonwealth as a whole suffered 466,045 deaths. Poland mourned the deaths of a staggering 5,675,000 inhabitants, around 20 per cent of its pre-war population. Many of these deaths can be attributed to Stalin.

A ruined building preserved as part of the memorial complex in Stalingrad (now Volgograd): in the background is a museum dedicated to those who fell in battle against the defeated German forces

mount a counter-offensive, which succeeded in encircling the German Sixth Army, forcing its surrender in January 1943. He oversaw the great tank battle at Kursk and then drove the German army all the way back to Berlin.

When Zhukov returned to Moscow in 1946, he was greeted as a great hero. But Stalin was a jealous man. He did not want to share the limelight with anyone. Zhukov was posted to Odessa, then the Urals, while Stalin took the credit for winning the Great Patriotic War.

The Katyn Affair

With the Soviet Union at war with Germany, Stalin had a problem – he was now allied to Poland, whose government in exile was in London. In August 1941 Stalin agreed to let a Polish army be formed on Soviet territory under General Wladyslaw Anders, who asked the Soviets to hand over the 15,000 Polish officers they had once held in camps at Smolensk. The Soviets stalled by telling Anders that most of the prisoners had escaped to Manchuria and could not be located, but on 13 April 1943 a German military force announced that it had discovered mass graves containing Polish officers in the Katyn Forest, near Smolensk. A total of 4,443 corpses were unearthed. Their hands were tied and they had been shot in the back of the head, piled up in stacks and then buried. Investigators determined that they were General Anders' missing officers who had been executed by the Soviets in 1940, according to the Germans. The Soviets then claimed that the Polish officers had been engaged in construction work to the west of Smolensk when the Germans arrived in August 1941 and that the German attackers had killed them. However, the Germans and the Red Cross produced evidence that the officers had been killed in 1940. The Soviet government refused to co-operate any further with the Red Cross investigators and on 25 April 1943 Russia broke off diplomatic relations with the Polish government in London. The Soviets then established a rival Polish government in exile, composed entirely of Communists.

The Soviet Union continued to insist that the Polish officers had been killed by the Germans and the Communist government installed in Warsaw after 1945 had no choice but to accept this story. However, when a non-communist collation came to power in Poland in 1989, its members shifted the blame on to the Soviets. Finally, in

April 1990 Soviet president Mikhail Gorbachev admitted that the NKVD, the Soviet secret police force, was responsible for the massacre. Two years later the original order, signed by Stalin, was handed over to the Polish government.

The Deportations Continue

While the war against Germany was raging, the deportations of ethnic minorities within the Soviet Union continued. The Kalmyks were a Mongolic people from south-west Russia, who were mainly Buddhists and Orthodox Christians. Accused of supplying cattle to the Germans, who had simply taken the livestock, they were deported to Central Asia and Siberia in 1943. Then half a million Muslim Chechens were imprisoned, beaten and deported. In 1944 they were followed by over 190,000 Tartars, who were removed from the Crimea, where they had lived for seven centuries. With them went the Greeks, the Armenians and the Bulgarians who lived in the area. The Soviets claimed that they had collaborated with the Germans who had occupied the Crimea, but there was no truth in the allegation.

As this account shows, the deportees had to endure untold misery.

'It was a journey of lingering death in cattle trucks, crammed with people, like mobile gas chambers. The journey lasted three to four weeks and took them across the scorching summer steppes of Kazakhstan. They took Red partisans of the Crimea, the fighters of the Bolshevik underground, and the Soviet and Party activists. Also invalids and old men. The remaining men were fighting at the front, but deportation awaited them at the end of the war. And in the meantime, they crammed their women and children into trucks, where they constituted the vast majority. Death mowed down the old, the young and the weak. They died of thirst, suffocation and the stench… On the long stages, the corpses decomposed in the huddle of the trucks, and at the short halts, where water and food were handed out, the people were not allowed to bury their dead and had to leave them beside the railway trucks.'

Then there is the harrowing testimony of a young woman who was deported on 18 May 1944.

'At 3 am, two soldiers knocked on the door. I was the eldest daughter. I had four younger sisters. The soldiers told us: "You've got fifteen minutes and then we are going to take you away." Our father reminded us about the Germans and how they had gone around collecting Jews and shooting them. He was convinced they were going to do the same to all of us. So he told us not to bother taking anything with us — that we were all going to be shot. So we left with only the clothes on our backs. It was only that night that they put the people from our village on to trucks and took us to the railway. When we arrived in Uzbekistan it was 43 degrees Celsius [110 degrees Fahrenheit] —

unimaginable heat. I was the only one to survive. My father, mother and sisters all perished from the ordeal.'

While the homes and the vineyards of the wealthier Tartars were given to Soviet officials as holiday villas, their deposed owners lived in windowless barracks, where they survived on 150 grams (five ounces) of bread a day. Many died in the accompanying typhus epidemic. The deportation was completed two weeks ahead of schedule so the man in charge, Beria's trusted henchman Bogdan Kobulov, threw a celebration party in Moscow. But then he discovered that a small community of Tartars was still living at Arabat Bay, in the south-west corner of the Sea of Azov. They were quickly rounded up and forced on to a boat, which was then taken out into the Sea of Azov and scuttled. Those who did not drown were machine-gunned.

The deportations were costly in terms of men and materials because troops and

As deportations continued, the Red Army grappled with the Nazis. Third from the left is Leonid Brezhnev, president of the USSR from 1964 to 1982: he was a political commissar as the 18th Army advanced through Ukraine in 1943

THE RAPE OF BERLIN

When Berlin fell, Stalin believed that his men should have their reward, so he encouraged them to celebrate. The Soviet troops went on an orgy of drinking, looting and raping. It is thought that as many as 100,000 women were raped – often publicly – during that period in Berlin, and an estimated two million in the whole of eastern Germany. Even Russian women who had been taken into Germany as slave labour were raped. Russian soldiers often shot their victims afterwards and other women committed suicide. In one district of Berlin alone, 215 female suicides were recorded in three weeks.

rolling stock had to be diverted from the front. After the death of Stalin it was admitted that there had also been plans to deport the whole of the population of Ukraine, which had been occupied by Germany early in the war, but the deportation did not go ahead because there were too many people to move.

Following the reconquest of the occupied territories, a special department was set up to root out 'traitors, deserters and cowards'. This was later incorporated into SMERSH – a contraction of *Smert Shpionam*, or 'Death to Spies' – the arch-enemy of James Bond. It was the creation of Stalin himself and it reported directly to him. Polish partisans who had been fighting the Germans were rounded up and seconded into Soviet-controlled units, or simply shot. The NKVD also penetrated the Red Army. In Stalin's eyes, no one in the military was to be trusted. NKVD officers wore the uniforms and insignia of the units they had been assigned to but everyone was aware of their chief function, which was to quash any hint of dissent, dissatisfaction or rumour-mongering. Indeed, NKVD units armed with machine guns followed Red Army infantry units into battle, just in case any soldiers thought twice about sacrificing their lives. The NKVD also punished offenders by sending them in to clear minefields.

Under Order 270, all Soviet soldiers who had surrendered were to be shot and their families terrorized. Deserters – even those who had simply got lost in the chaos of war – were also summarily executed. Anyone who had been captured and had escaped was sent to an NKVD Special Camp. Senior Lieutenant Mikhail Petrovich Deviataev was a Soviet fighter pilot who had shot down nine enemy planes before being captured. Keen to get back into action, he escaped from a prisoner of war camp, hijacked a German bomber and flew back to the Soviet lines. His reward was 12 years in the Gulag.

The Warsaw Uprising

As the Red Army approached Warsaw in July 1944, Stalin encouraged the Polish Home Army, who numbered about 50,000, to rise up against the Germans. Loyal to the Polish government in exile in London, they were eager to do so before the Soviets entered the city because Moscow was already preparing its own Communist-led government to take over in Poland. The Home Army attacked the German garrison on 1 August and within three days it had taken over most of the city. However, the approaching Red Army stopped when it reached the banks of the Vistula.

If the Home Army had expected assistance from the Soviets they were mistaken. Stalin was playing a devious game of his own. The Soviets' inaction enabled the Germans to send in reinforcements so that the uprising could be put down unhindered.

Not only was there no assistance from Stalin, but he also blocked supplies to the beleaguered Poles by refusing the Western Allies permission to use Soviet airfields. And Home Army reinforcements were disarmed by the Soviets when they tried to enter the city. Without ammunition and food, the Home Army was forced to surrender on 2 October, after an epic 63-day struggle. An escaped prisoner of war who joined the Home Army in Warsaw gave this account.

> 'About half the population have been wounded or killed. Almost every soldier, if not killed, has received a wound of some sort. The population shelter in cellars, which often become collective graves... In the large concentration camp on the city's outskirts there are tens of thousands of Polish people who are starving to death... All Polish military prisoners who fall into German hands are murdered.'

Survivors were deported and the city was destroyed.

Once the destruction of the city was complete, the Red Army resumed its advance. And when the Germans were finally driven out of Poland, the way was open for Stalin to install his own pro-Soviet regime on 1 January 1945. What remained of the Home Army broke up into autonomous units and joined the resistance. But Stalin would brook no opposition. Beria invited the head of the Home Army, General Leopold Okulicki, and seven leading resistance leaders to accompany 'General Ivanov' to London for meetings with the British, American and Soviet representatives.

But there was no General Ivanov. Instead, the Polish leaders were flown to Moscow, where they were taken to the Lubyanka for interrogation. On 18 June 1945, Okulicki and 15 other leading Poles went on trial for collaborating with the Germans against the Soviets – though Okulicki had led the Warsaw Uprising. He was sentenced to ten years' imprisonment, but he was murdered in jail in 1946. Communist rule in Poland was only relinquished in 1989.

The Aftermath of War

While the Allies sought to rebuild the shattered infrastructure of western Germany, the Soviets were determined to extract reparations: so they transported machinery and entire factories back to Soviet soil, impoverishing East Germany for the next 50

Heroic Soviet troops are welcomed by grateful Polish villagers in this propaganda shot of 1944. The reality was different, however, and Stalin's ruthless tactics produced an abiding Polish hatred of the Russians for years to come

years. Nine NKVD regiments and 500 SMERSH operatives were then sent to East Prussia. Fifty thousand 'enemy elements' had already been rounded up there between January and April 1945. The land was laid waste, low-lying areas were reduced to swamp and farmers were forced to abandon livestock, which was either slaughtered or transported to the Soviet Union. The remaining civilians – largely women and girls – were deported to inhospitable regions, where they were forced to work for up to 16 hours a day.

To the west, the British kept the weapons that had been impounded from the Germans close to the prisoners of war, in case it was necessary to re-arm them. The advancing Russians had deceived the British prisoners of war from the east by telling them that they were on their way to London instead of Berlin, their true destination. It seems that Stalin had designs on western Europe as well as the eastern section that the Red Army already occupied. He was only dissuaded from continuing his advance

by the large American force on the Continent and the massive air superiority of the Anglo-American alliance.

At a meeting between Stalin, Churchill and Roosevelt in Yalta in February 1945, it had been agreed that there would be free elections in Poland, Czechoslovakia, Hungary, Romania and Bulgaria. Instead, Stalin installed pro-Soviet governments.

'A freely elected government in any of these countries would be anti-Soviet,' said Stalin with implacable logic, 'and that we cannot allow.'

As those countries were already occupied by the Red Army, there was nothing that the Western democracies could do about it. This was particularly galling for the British, because they had gone to war to guarantee Poland's freedom in the first place. Fifteen NKVD regiments were sent into Poland, where they took over the Ministry of Public Security. The post-war frontiers of Poland had been decided by a meeting between Stalin, Churchill and Roosevelt at Tehran in November 1943. Stalin insisted on taking a slice of eastern Poland 185 miles (300 km) wide. In compensation, Poland would move its western border to a line that ran along the Oder and Neisse rivers, while the northern part of East Prussia was annexed by the Soviet Union. The Western Allies objected, but when they met Stalin again at the Potsdam conference in July 1945 the territory was already occupied by the Red Army. The Germans who lived there were deported and when a formal peace treaty was signed between the Soviet-dominated German Democratic Republic – commonly known as East Germany – and Poland, the Oder-Neisse line was recognized as the border.

Stalin insisted that all Soviet prisoners of war who were liberated from prisoner of war camps by the British and the Americans must be returned to the Soviet Union, along with Soviet concentration camp inmates, slave labourers and turncoats. They would be sent to the Gulag. Stalin was particularly eager to get his hands on the Cossacks. Before the Revolution they had been used by the tsar to put down insurrections and, during the Russian Civil War, they had fought on the side of the

Whites. They had suffered particularly badly during the collectivization period, having being driven from their fertile land. Many had left the country. Those that remained were jubilant when the Germans invaded, because they hoped that this would mark the end of Soviet rule. By 1944, over 250,000 Cossacks were serving with the German army, many of them in anti-partisan units.

In the summer of 1945, SMERSH agents in Austria found 50,000 Cossack and White Russians, including 11,000 women and children. With them were two White generals, 75-year-old Peter Krasnow and Andre Shkuro. They had surrendered to the British and the Soviets demanded that they be handed over. Harold Macmillan, Minister of State, Mediterranean, and political adviser to Field Marshal Sir Harold Alexander, British commander in the field, wrote,

> 'To hand them over to the Russians is condemning them to slavery, torture and probably death. To refuse, is deeply to offend the Russians, and incidentally break the Yalta Agreement.'

In fact, many of the Cossacks had French or Yugoslav citizenship, or were stateless, because they had left Russia during the Revolution, before the establishment of the Soviet state, so had never been Soviet citizens. However, Alexander decided to hand them over because the Soviets were holding 15,597 American and 8,462 British prisoners of war, recently liberated from prisoner of war camps. There was to be an exchange.

'It had to be done,' said Macmillan. 'We had no power to stop it. And not to do it would have meant they would have not sent back our British prisoners.'

The Cossacks were handed over at gunpoint. Most rapidly disappeared into the Gulag, while Krasnow and other leaders were sent for 'special treatment' in the cellars of the Lubyanka. After prolonged periods of torture and humiliation they were killed. Meanwhile the British and American prisoners of war in Austria were heading eastwards in cattle trucks. This was after the repatriation point in Odessa had been closed.

In all 31,000 British and Commonwealth soldiers and 20,000 Americans ended up in the Gulag, along with 250,000 French, 85,000 Belgian and 4,000 Dutch

Red Army soldiers march through a Russian town ready to take on the Germans. These troops were essentially cannon fodder, fed into the Soviet war machine with minimal chances of emerging unscathed on the other side

troops – not to mention Italians, Romanians, Bulgarians, Hungarians and Spaniards, who had been fighting for the other side. Stalin was particularly keen to hold on to Allied airmen. He did not trust Churchill, who was a long-standing enemy of the Soviet state. As secretary of war, Churchill had been behind the Allied intervention in 1919. With the collapse of Nazi Germany, Churchill was convinced that war with the Soviet Union was inevitable. As the Red Army advanced, the British placed agents behind their lines so that they would be able to disrupt communications when the expected Anglo-Soviet war began.

The man in charge of this operation was the double agent Kim Philby, so Stalin was well aware of Churchill's intentions. He was not about to hand back airmen who might be dropping bombs on Moscow a few weeks later. Captured Allied airmen were also seen in factories, working on advanced radar equipment. At the time, the priority was to ensure that the Soviet Union joined in the war against Japan, so requests for the return of Allied prisoners of war ceased. By the time the war with Japan was over the Cold War had begun and the missing prisoners of war were written off. A handful escaped after Stalin's death in 1953 and, when they returned to their home countries, they were held for prolonged 'debriefs' and then sworn to secrecy before they were released.

When the United Nations set up an Ad Hoc Commission on Prisoners of War in 1946, the West German government complained that there were 1,300,000 German prisoners missing – 1,200,000 from the Eastern Front. Furthermore, some 750,000 German civilians had been taken into the Soviet Union, while 8,243 were still detained in Czechoslovakia and 8,910, including 3,240 children, were held in Poland. When the Ad Hoc Commission was wound up in 1957 only 22,457 prisoners had been returned. The rest had disappeared into Stalin's slave labour system, where they died.

JAPANESE PRISONERS

Japanese prisoners of war were treated as badly as their German counterparts – and the Russian inmates of the Gulag. They were starved, denied medical attention, forced to work and maltreated. Many died. This was not random brutality. It was part of a well thought out plan. Those who survived the first winter were strong enough to perform the hard work that was valuable to the Soviet economy. And it was not just prisoners of war who suffered. Some 26,000 Japanese civilians were also captured in Korea.

In 1947, older prisoners, the injured and the sick were returned to Japan. The younger ones were then subjected to indoctrination. Group criticism, self-criticism and denouncements set prisoner against prisoner.

Some were lynched and others were trampled to death. When the surviving Japanese prisoners of war were eventually sent home they had become diehard Communists. In one instance, the captain of a ship carrying them back to Japan was tried by a kangaroo court. The returning prisoners of war refused to fill in landing cards and they staged demonstrations on the dockside. They also made unplanned stops on their way home, so that they could attend Communist rallies, and 400 ex-prisoners of war forced their way into the Diet, Japan's parliament. It was all part of Stalin's plan to deliver the core of a powerful communist party into what was to become one of the world's most successful capitalist nations.

United Nations servicemen captured during the Korean War were subjected to similar indoctrination and some, such as the British spy George Blake, were successfully recruited as double agents.

CHAPTER TEN

THE IRON CURTAIN

Two of the 'Big Three' war leaders were no longer in power at the end of the Second World War. First of all, President Roosevelt died on 12 April 1945. He was replaced by Harry S. Truman, who had been vice-president for just 82 days. And during the Potsdam Conference that began in July, Winston Churchill was replaced as prime minister by the considerably less forceful Clement Attlee. Only Stalin remained and he saw no reason at all why he should not go on to dominate the world.

Attlee, Truman and Stalin at the Potsdam conference in 1945 which met to redraw the map of Europe. Truman also told Stalin about the successful testing of 'a new weapon of unusual destructive force', the atomic bomb

At A VICTORY PARADE ON **24 JUNE 1945**, SOVIET TROOPS THREW CAPTURED NAZI BANNERS AT STALIN'S FEET AS HE STOOD ON TOP OF LENIN'S MAUSOLEUM IN THE POURING RAIN. He was made a 'Hero of the Soviet Union' and promoted to the rank of generalissimo. The official line was that the pre-war policies of enforced collectivization and industrialization based on slave labour were justified by the victory against Nazi Germany, even though it had cost 20 million deaths.

However, the war had crippled the Soviet Union. Millions had died, millions more were homeless and much of the country's industrial capacity had been destroyed and its infrastructure wrecked. In 1948, the United States Congress approved an economic recovery plan for Europe that had been proposed by Secretary of State George C. Marshall. Over the next four years, the Marshall Plan distributed 13 billion dollars to Austria, Belgium, Denmark, France, Greece, Iceland, Ireland, Italy, Luxembourg, The Netherlands, Norway, Portugal, Sweden, Switzerland, Turkey, the United Kingdom and West Germany. But the Soviet Union withdrew from the plan at an early stage, preferring to go its own way. Under orders from Moscow the eastern European states under occupation followed suit. The Cold War was now under way.

On 5 March 1946, Winston Churchill made a speech in Fulton, Missouri, in which he issued the following warning.

'From Stettin in the Baltic to Trieste in the Adriatic, an iron curtain has descended across Europe.'

The armies of occupation of Britain, France and the United States faced the Red Army in an uneasy stand-off. Meanwhile, Stalin began tightening security at home. In March 1946 the NKVD was elevated to ministerial status as the MVD – *Ministerstvo Vnutrennikh Del* or Ministry of Internal Affairs. Its sister organization, the wartime NKGB – *Narodnyi Kommissariat Gosudarstvennoi Bezopasnosti* or People's Commissariat for State Security, which controlled the armed forces and co-operated in the deportations – became the MGB – *Ministerstvo Gosudarstvennoi Bezopasnosti* or Ministry of State Security, with Viktor Abakumov as its first chief. It specialized in espionage and counter-espionage and was involved in the suppression of nationalists in the Baltic states, Belorussia and Ukraine. Partisan groups that had grown up to fight the Germans during the war were seen as a particular threat. MGB partisan groups were set up alongside them as *agents provocateurs* and when the nationalists showed their true colours they were destroyed. In some areas, this struggle went on until 1952.

After the war, the Gulag filled up again, notably with women who were accused of sleeping with the Germans. Inmates who had hoped for an amnesty at the end of the hostilities were

A notoriously brutal head of the MGB, Abakumov joined the Soviet security services in 1932 and was transferred to the OGPU headquarters in the Lubyanka in the following year. In 1934, he joined the directorate of the Gulag where he survived the Great Purge by becoming one of its willing executioners. Four years later, in 1938, he joined the NKVD, where he rose to a high position. When the new NKGB was created in 1941, he became one of Beria's deputies. After Germany attacked the Soviet Union, Stalin ordered Abakumov to deal with the Red Army commanders who had been accused of betrayal or cowardice. His efficient methods enabled him to become one of Stalin's deputies and he was made head of the Chief Counterintelligence Directorate of the People's Commissariat of Defence of the USSR, better known as SMERSH, when it was created in April 1943. In 1946 the NKGB became the MGB and Stalin personally appointed Abakumov as head of the organization. He used his position to indulge his passion for torture while using MGB funds to maintain a string of mistresses. In 1949 he organized the purge known as the 'Leningrad Affair', but his triumph was short-lived. He was arrested on Stalin's orders in 1951 and confined to a refrigerated cell. Stalin's death did not improve his position. On 18 December 1954 he was shot for his involvement in the Leningrad Affair.

Dmitri Shostakovich who was regularly humiliated by Zhdanov

disappointed, because their 'release' meant nothing beyond a stamp on a piece of paper. They were forced to settle in the region of the camp and they still had to continue the work they had been assigned to. Few ever saw their homes again.

Cultural Purge

Artists and writers were particularly at risk in the post-war era. Stalin initiated a cultural purge under Andrei Zhdanov, who introduced a strict ideological code called 'Zhdanovism'. Initially it was directed at two literary magazines, *Zvezda* and *Leninigrad*, which published the apolitical writing of the satirist Mikhail Mikhailovich Zoshchenko and the poet Anna Akhmatova. The writers were accused of being bourgeois individualists before being expelled from the Union of Soviet Writers. Literature, Zhdanov insisted, was for 'the education of labouring people in the spirit of socialism'. Zoshchenko died in poverty in 1958, while Akhmatova's prominence increased until her death in 1966. When her son was sent to the Gulag she wrote poetry in praise of Stalin in order to secure his release, but much of her work was still directed against the Soviet system.

'Ideologically impure' work was banned from all Soviet libraries, as well as new and second-hand bookshops. The composer Dmitri Shostakovich suffered particularly badly under Zhdanov, who presumed to tinkle out on the piano what he held to be acceptable 'people's tunes'. Shostakovich was forced to recant on several occasions, but he still expected to be apprehended at any moment. In fact, he waited on the landing at night so his family would not be disturbed if he was arrested. Eventually he wrote a piece that the Soviet Committee on Art approved of. His oratorio *Song of the Forests*, they said, 'sings of the peaceful work of the Soviet people in realizing the great Stalinist

Anna Akhmatova was forced to write poetry in praise of Stalin when her son was consigned to the Gulag

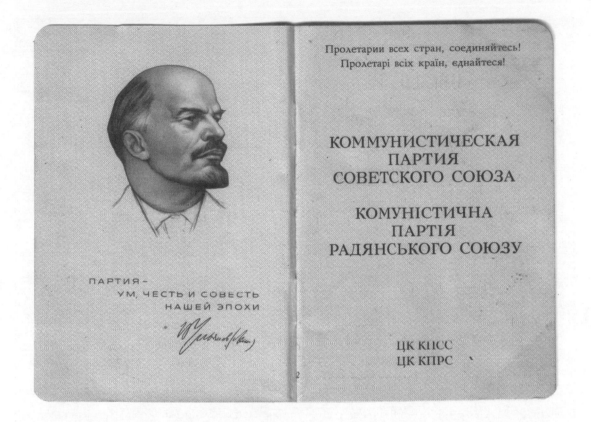

A Communist Party card: some comrades were more equal than others and card-carrying members were entitled to a range of privileges, including access to shops with foreign goods, holiday packages, foreign travel, housing and jobs

plan'. At the time, Stalin had decided to tackle drought by creating forest belts across the Soviet Union's richest farming areas. Visitors to art galleries were given official guides and exhibition notes provided by the All-Union Arts Committee set up by Stalin. Anything that did not follow the precepts of 'Socialist Realism' was ousted. Literary critics were denounced for suggesting that Russian classics had been influenced by Lord Byron, Charles Dickens, Jean-Jacques Rousseau or Molière. Under Zhdanovism, Western scientific theories and inventions were claimed as Russian.

The death of Zhdanov in 1948 was followed by a new purge known as the 'Leningrad Affair'. As well as heading the Communist Party of Leningrad, Zhdanov had been the rival of Georgy Malenkov, who was supported by Lavrenty Beria.

It is thought by some that Malenkov was trying to eliminate any threat to his position by claiming that Zhdanov's supporters in Leningrad were trying to create a rival Communist Party. The purge spread into the Russian Soviet Federated Socialist Republic and resulted in the imprisonment and execution of thousands of party officials and managers. Others have suggested that Stalin initiated the purge himself, in order to remove the rising young leaders of the Leningrad faction. Nevertheless, Zhdanov's campaign condemning 'Westernism' or 'cosmopolitanism' continued until Stalin's death in 1953.

ANDREI ALEXANDROVICH ZHDANOV (1896–1948)

After joining the Bolsheviks in 1915, Zhdanov became a close associate of Stalin and took over as head of the Party in Leningrad after the death of Sergey Kirov in 1934. He participated in the Great Purge, when he personally approved 176 execution lists, and in 1940 he was sent to oversee the annexation of Estonia. During the Great Patriotic War he was in charge of the defence of Leningrad, where over a million civilians lost their lives, along with some two and a half million Soviet troops. With the fall of Nazi Germany and its ally, Finland, he became head of the Allied Control Commission in Helsinki. Allied Control Commissions were established in all of the occupied countries.

After the war, Zhdanov's son Yuri became Svetlana Stalin's second husband. In 1947, Zhdanov organized the Cominform, which was designed to co-ordinate Communist parties throughout Europe. Turning to the arts, in February 1948 he initiated purges within the musical world. Dmitri Shostakovich, Sergei Prokofiev, Aram Khachaturian and many other composers were reprimanded during this period. Stalin had talked of Zhdanov being his successor, but Zhdanov's ill health gave his rivals, Beria and Malenkov, an opportunity to undermine him. In 1948 Zhdanov died of heart failure in Moscow, though Khrushchev said he could not control his drinking. There have been allegations that Zhdanov's failure to organize a Communist takeover in Finland resulted in Stalin ordering his death.

The Communist Takeover

ROMANIA

While Stalin was reimposing the rule of the iron fist inside the Soviet Union, he was also building an iron empire outside it. The first of Germany's allies to leave the Axis was Romania. Hitler and Stalin had already annexed one third of the territory of Romania and they partitioned it between them in the summer of 1940. The fascist dictator Ion Antonescu, who was Hitler's puppet, then took over as prime minister. Antonescu declared war on the Soviet Union in 1941, but as losses mounted on the Eastern Front, he became increasingly unpopular. Opposition came from the National Democratic Block, which was led by the National Peasant Party. Within it

Romanian dictator Ion Antonescu is arrested: responsible for the deaths of some 400,000 Jews, Antonescu was briefly detained in the Soviet Union before being returned to a people's tribunal in Romania and executed

was the National Democratic Front (FND) which comprised the Communist Party, the Social Democrats and two smaller left-wing parties.

In August 1944, as the Romanian army pulled back through Moldova, King Michael of Romania called Antonescu and his foreign minister to the palace and ordered them to conclude an armistice with the Allies. When they demurred, he had them arrested and at 22.00 hours Bucharest Radio broadcast an order to all Romanian forces telling them to cease hostilities. Hitler then ordered the *Luftwaffe* to bomb Bucharest. Romania responded by declaring war on Germany. All of the Danube crossings were seized and opened to the Red Army.

Once the Yalta Conference was over, Stalin sent Andrei Vyshinsky to Bucharest, where he ordered King Michael to form an FND government under Petru Groza, founder of an agrarian organization known as the Ploughmen's Front. Under pressure from the United States and Britain, Groza agreed to call elections, though he did not promise to abide by the results.

'If the reactionaries succeed,' he said, 'we shall immediately take our revenge.'

Another member of his government, Gheorghe Tătărescu, threatened to countenance no opposition.

'We shall put some in prison,' he said, 'liquidate others and the rest we shall immediately deport.'

After the Communists took over, Tătărescu met the fate he had decreed for

REPUBLICA POPULARA ROMANA

SLAVĂ MARELUI STALIN!

11 LEI POSTA

Stalin portrayed himself as a lover of children, but Svetlana said he had little interest in his grandchildren

others by being arrested and imprisoned. In the run-up to the election, censorship was tightened by clamping down on the newspaper and radio stations. Members of the opposition parties were arrested, their officials were harassed and their meetings were stormed. Before the polling stations opened government supporters were allowed to vote several times and during the count the telephone lines to opposition strongholds were cut, thereby giving Party members time to falsify the returns. When that was done, the FND declared that it had won by an 80 per cent majority.

At a meeting in Moscow the United States protested, insisting that Groza should appoint members of the opposition to his cabinet. Stalin conceded the point and Groza appointed two members from other left-wing parties. Even then, they were given no portfolios. The Communist Party then moved against the National Peasant Party, which had previously been the biggest faction in the National Democratic Block. Members were put under house arrest before being sentenced to penal servitude.

On 30 December 1947 the Elisabeta Palace in Bucharest was surrounded by a Soviet-raised Romanian division and King Michael was forced to abdicate – or face charges of conspiring with Britain and the United States against his own government. The Communist Party general secretary and hard-line Stalinist Gheorghe Gheorghiu-Dej then attacked the fiery foreign minister, Anna Pauker, herself a hard-line Communist, on the grounds that she was a 'Jewess of bourgeois origin'. What was required, he said, was someone 'from the ranks of the working class, a true-born Romanian'. Stalin then condemned her 'peasantist, non-Marxist policies'. She was arrested and charged with 'cosmopolitanism' – a charge that Stalin often levelled against Jews. However, she survived the death of Stalin and was allowed to live in retirement. Meanwhile Gheorghiu-Dej took power and formed a Communist one-party state along Stalinist lines.

BULGARIA

Bulgaria joined the Second World War on the Axis side on 1 March 1941 and the nation participated in the invasion of Yugoslavia and Greece. However, King Boris III refused to join in the attack on the Soviet Union, which he saw as a traditional ally. This infuriated Hitler and the two men had an acrimonious meeting. Shortly afterwards, on 28 August 1943, King Boris died in mysterious circumstances. Needless to say, conspiracy theories abound. The king's son, Simeon II, was only a child so a three-man regency council took control. Realizing that the war was going against Germany, the council began peace negotiations with London and Washington, but it was too late. Stalin saw Bulgaria as part of the Soviet sphere of influence, so he declared war on 5 September 1944. Bulgaria retorted by declaring war on Germany. Peace negotiations were then transferred to Moscow, where an armistice was signed on 28 October.

Soviet troops invade Bulgaria in 1944: Stalin had long coveted Bulgaria and had been conducting a campaign of sedition and espionage against the Axis allies since 1941. Finally, he orchestrated the overthrow of the government

Meanwhile the Red Army entered Bulgaria and the Communist-dominated Fatherland Front took over in Sofia. The three members of the regency council were then put in front of a firing squad – naked, because the authorities did not want to damage their clothes. However, Simeon II survived. He lived in exile in Madrid for 50 years and then returned to Bulgaria. He was elected prime minister as Simeon Saxe-Coburg-Gotha in 2001.

Although the Communists were not the largest faction in the Fatherland Front, the minister of the interior and the minister of justice were both Party members. They set up People's Courts to purge those behind Bulgaria's earlier pro-German stance. By February 1945, over 2,600 people had been sentenced to death and another 1,100 had been imprisoned for life. A further 4,300 defendants were imprisoned for shorter periods. Nikola Petkov, the leader of the Agrarian Party, refused to co-operate with the Communists and was executed in 1947.

The way was now clear for the leader of the Communist Party, Georgi Dimitrov, to return from exile in Moscow and take over as prime minister, while keeping his Soviet citizenship. He tried to form an alliance with Marshal Tito in Yugoslavia, but he fell out of favour when Stalin and Tito broke off relations. In July 1949 Dimitrov died in a sanatorium near Moscow. He was thought to have been poisoned. A team of interrogators under Lev Shvartsman, an agent trusted by Stalin, was sent to Bulgaria. Their task was to dispose of a number of Stalin's personal enemies. Deputy Prime

Georgi Dimitrov [above left with Marshal Fyodor Tolbukhin] was among the Communists tried by the Germans in 1933 for burning down the Reichstag, but he ran rings round prosecutor Hermann Goering and was freed

JOSIP BROZ TITO (1892–1980)

Born to a large peasant family in Croatia, Josip Broz was conscripted into the Austro-Hungarian army in 1913 and served on the Russian front, where he was wounded and captured in 1915. After the Revolution he joined the Red Guard in Omsk, Siberia. After marrying a Russian woman, he returned to Croatia in 1920, when he joined the Communist Party of Yugoslavia, which was soon banned.

Always militant, he led demonstrations following the assassination of Croat deputies in the Belgrade parliament in June 1928. Bombs were found in his flat when he was arrested two months later and he was sentenced to five years' imprisonment. When he was released, he joined the Politburo in Vienna and began using the pseudonym 'Tito' for underground work.

In 1935 and 1936, Tito [*seen above with a bemedalled Leonid Brezhnev*] worked with the Comintern in Moscow and then he returned to underground work in Yugoslavia. When the Axis powers, led by Italy and Germany, invaded Yugoslavia in April 1941 the Communists became partisans. In 1943, the Western Allies recognized Tito as the leader of the resistance in Yugoslavia and his forces were supplied by Britain. However, it was the Red Army that liberated the country in late 1944 and early 1945. Tito then took over. The country was remodelled along Soviet lines. Stalin tried to topple Tito in 1948, but he managed to hold on to power. The West offered Yugoslavia aid and military assistance and Tito formed an informal association with NATO. Unwilling to give up on a one-party dictatorship, Tito sought a reconciliation with Nikita Khrushchev, but the relationship cooled following the Soviet interventions in Hungary in 1956 and Czechoslovakia in 1960. Tito pursued a policy of non-alignment from then on. His death in 1980 led to Yugoslavia being broken up into its constituent parts.

Minister Traicho Kostov was hanged in December 1949, scores of others were sent to prison and the Social Democrats were forced to merge with the Communist Party.

HUNGARY

Hungary joined the Axis powers in August 1940, but the regent, Admiral Miklós Horthy, was seen as an unreliable ally. However, when Germany occupied Hungary on 27 March 1944 Horthy was kept in power, even though he opposed the deportation of the Jews. But Horthy could see that Germany had lost the war so he secretly contacted London and Washington, who insisted that he negotiate an armistice with Moscow. Accordingly, on 11 October Hungary agreed to an immediate cessation of hostilities. However, the Hungarian Third Army fought on. On 13 February 1945, Budapest fell to the Red Army. With them came Hungarian Communist Gabor Peter, who had set up the Political Police a month before. In order to fund his secret police force Peter began to blackmail Janos Kessmenn, a Hungarian Nazi whose job had been to ship Jews to the death camps. When that was no longer possible he lined them up on the quays of the Danube, where he shot them and pushed their bodies into the water. Kessmenn had been stealing from his victims and he handed over $90,000 in foreign exchange, 1,500 carats of diamonds and over 10,000 gold items.

Peter also took to straightforward robbery and extortion. Those who would not

Grigory Vorozheikin with Marshal Seymon Timoshenko in Budapest in 1945: Vorozheikin was a Soviet Airforce general and Timoshenko was one of the Red Army's top soldiers, having survived Stalin's regular purges

co-operate were handed over to the NKVD. He then established the AVO – *Allamvedelmi Osztaly* or State Security Authority. This private army had limitless powers and was under the control of the Communist Party. Once the country was cleared of Germans, Moscow installed a provisional government and elections were held. They were won by the Smallholders' Party, who gained 57 per cent of the vote. However, the chairman of the Allied Control Commission, Marshal Kliment Voroshilov, sidelined the British and American members and established a coalition government where Communists held all the key posts.

László Rajik, the minister of the interior who controlled Peter's AVO, began to hold show trials. But this provoked the jealousy of Mátyás Rákosi, the Stalinist head of the Hungarian Working People's Party (MDP). The MDP was formed when the Communists forced the Social Democrats to merge with them. Rajik was forced from office and then he was arrested on the charge of being a 'Titoist spy'. After being tortured, he was told that his life would be spared if he confessed during a show trial. Anxious to live he did as he was asked, but he was still executed, along with the 17 people who had stood trial with him. Further show trials decimated the Smallholders' Party.

Janos Kádár, a friend of Rajik's who had been complicit in his torture, trial and execution, replaced him as minister of the interior. The following year Kádár himself was arrested, beaten and charged with being a Titoist. At his show trial he was found guilty and sentenced to life imprisonment, though he only served three years of his term. Gabor Peter, who was Jewish, fell from power during Stalin's anti-Semitic purges of the early 1950s. He too was sentenced to life imprisonment for 'crimes against the state and the people', but he was released in 1959 and allowed to work as a tailor and a librarian.

It was estimated that 2,000 people were executed and 100,000 more were imprisoned during the purge of Hungary. Apolitical organizations such as the Boy Scouts and the Catholic Youth were disbanded and Catholic schools were nationalized. Cardinal József Mindszenty, who had been imprisoned by the Nazis, opposed these actions and condemned Communism as an atheistic ideology. He was arrested and interrogated. Stripped of his cardinal's robes, he was beaten and humiliated, while being fed mind-altering drugs. Then charges were concocted against him. Urging Catholics to hold on to their churches, schools and land was denounced as sabotaging land reform, accepting aid from American sources brought currency charges, while making speeches condemning Communism was treason. Now a broken man, Mindszenty confessed during a show trial in February 1949. He was sentenced to life imprisonment, but he was freed by the Hungarian Uprising in 1956. When the Communists regained power, he sought asylum in the United States Embassy in Budapest, where he remained for 15 years. In 1971 he moved to Vienna, where he died in 1975.

CZECHOSLOVAKIA

Czechoslovakia was the only Soviet-occupied country to which the government in exile was allowed to return. Forced from office by the Munich agreement in 1938, Edvard Beneš returned to Prague in triumph in May 1945. He brought with him his foreign minister, the immensely popular Jan Masaryk, son of Tomáš Masaryk, the first president of an independent Czechoslovakia. Beneš knew that he had to make concessions to Moscow, so he appointed a number of Communists to his cabinet. In July 1946 he made the leader of the Communist Party, Klement Gottwald, prime minister.

In 1947, Masaryk and Gottwald were summoned to Moscow by Stalin. They were told that Czechoslovakia would not be allowed to participate in the Marshall Plan, which Stalin saw as a threat to the Soviet control of eastern Europe.

On his return to Prague, Masaryk said, 'I left a minister of a sovereign state, but had come back as Stalin's lackey.'

In the following February, Gottwald forced Beneš to accept a Communist-dominated cabinet. Masaryk remained at his post but on 10 March 1948 his body, barefoot and clad in pyjamas, was found beneath the bathroom window of his foreign office apartment in Prague's Czernin Palace. It has never been established whether he had committed suicide or had been thrown out. Suspiciously, the telephone line to his apartment had been cut and details of forthcoming events were found in his diary. In 1993 a former NKVD agent said that she had heard colleagues boasting of Masaryk's murder after he had tried to escape along a window ledge.

Beneš refused to sign the new constitution and he died a broken man later that year. When Klement Gottwald became president of Czechoslovakia in June 1948 he imposed a Soviet government that was based on the Stalinist model. The names of friends and enemies alike were given to the NKVD.

Nicknamed 'The Meat Queue' by locals, this 50-metre-high, 17,000-tonne statue of Stalin in Prague was destroyed on Moscow's orders in 1962

Purges followed in the 1950s, which were accompanied by the judicial execution of some 180 Party officials, including the first secretary Rudolf Slánský, Gottwald's rival. Gottwald himself caught a chill at Stalin's funeral on 9 March 1953 and died of pneumonia five days later.

A Divided Berlin

Churchill's 'iron curtain' ran right across Germany, following the border between the British, American and French zone of occupation in the west and the Soviet zone to the east. Roughly corresponding to the line where the Red Army met the armies of the Western Allies in 1945, this became the frontier between capitalist West Germany and Communist East Germany. However, Berlin lay a hundred miles or so inside the Soviet zone. Under the Yalta agreement the city was divided into four zones of occupation, like Germany itself. East Berlin was in the Soviet zone, while the British, Americans and the French occupied the western half.

But Stalin did not want this enclave of Western capitalism to remain in the midst of what he saw as his territory. On 24 June 1948, he announced that the four-power agreement regarding Berlin was at an end and the Western Allies no longer had any right there. Stalin aimed to starve the city into surrender, so the Soviets cut off all road, rail and water links between Berlin and the West. But the British and the Americans began an airlift, supplying the city with planes that took off day and night. The state of tension grew and by mid-July the Red Army had transferred 40 divisions to East Germany, which faced just eight divisions in the Allied sector. In response, three groups of United States strategic bombers were sent as reinforcements to Britain. The Cold War threatened to become hot.

Despite shortages of fuel and electricity West Berlin survived, thanks to the airlift. On 12 May 1949 the Soviets lifted the blockade, though the airlift continued until 30 September. In all, 2,323,738 tons of food, fuel, machinery and other supplies had been flown in. The deployment of United States strategic bombers seemed to be a key factor in the failure of the blockade.

The Race for the Bomb

If Stalin's confrontation with the West was to be successful, it was vital that the Soviet Union develop an atomic bomb. Atomic physics was a field in which the Soviets had lagged behind the West. Influenced by Trofim Lysenko in the early 1930s, Soviet scientists had avoided the discipline because it was thought to be too theoretical and impractical. But with the late 1930s came the discovery of nuclear fission and Soviet physicists, like physicists all over the world, realized that vast amounts of energy could be released by splitting the uranium atom – though any practical application seemed decades away.

The Soviets were then treated to an information windfall. In 1941 John

Cairncross, one of the Cambridge spy ring, told his NKVD controller that a British government committee was about to submit a report to the war cabinet in which it would be shown that a mass of enriched uranium could be made to generate a nuclear chain reaction that would result in a very large explosion. Beria was later informed that the theoretical problems of building an atomic bomb had been 'fundamentally solved'. Then in April 1942, Soviet nuclear physicist Georgy Nikolayevich Flyorov informed Stalin that since the discovery of nuclear fission in 1939, Germany, Britain and America had published nothing on

Silence that speaks volumes: nuclear physicist Georgy Flyorov had worked out that the Allies were busy building an atomic bomb

nuclear physics. This led him to believe that they were working on an atomic bomb.

A Soviet atomic bomb project was set up under Vyacheslav Molotov, then foreign minister, but by 1944 responsibility for the programme was transferred to Lavrenty Beria, head of the NKVD, because it had become increasingly dependent on intelligence.

The NKVD already had an agent in place. In 1937, a member of the Communist Party of Great Britain, Melita Norwood, obtained a job with the British Non-Ferrous Metals Research Association – a cover for atomic research – in Euston, north London. And Soviet military intelligence, the GRU or *Glavnoye Razvedyvatel'noye Upravleniye*, had Klaus Fuchs.

A member of the German Communist Party, Fuchs fled Germany when the Nazis came to power in 1933. He then studied at the University of Edinburgh, where he earned his doctorate. After being briefly interned at the beginning of the Second World War, he was then released to do research on the Tubes Alloy project at

THE CAMBRIDGE FIVE

The term 'Cambridge Five' refers to a ring of spies who were recruited at Cambridge University in the 1930s. Its members – Kim Philby, Donald Maclean, Guy Burgess, Anthony Blunt and John Cairncross – were committed Communists who concealed their allegiance when they joined the British intelligence services. During the Second World War they passed secret information to the Soviet Union. In 1951 Burgess and Maclean disappeared, eventually resurfacing in Moscow, and Philby defected to the Soviet Union in 1963. In the following year, Blunt made a full confession in exchange for immunity from prosecution. He was publicly unmasked in 1979.

Because of information supplied by KGB agent Anatoliy Golitsyn, who defected in 1961, British intelligence were aware that the spy ring consisted of five members.

However, the water was muddied in 1962 when it was discovered that John Vassall, an Admiralty clerk and a homosexual, had been blackmailed into spying for the KGB. But then it emerged that he was merely a low-ranking source who had been sacrificed to protect a bigger fish, John Cairncross, who admitted to spying when incriminating papers were found in his possession in 1951. Anthony Blunt also identified Cairncross as the fifth man in 1964. However, other candidates include Sir Roger Hollis, who was head of MI5 at the time.

Birmingham University, a cover for the British nuclear weapons directorate. He became a British citizen in 1942. Even by 1941 he realized that the project he was working on would be of interest to the Soviet Union, so he contacted underground members of the German Communist Party. They put him on to Simon Davidovich Kremer, an officer of the GRU who was secretary to the Soviet military attaché in London. In the following summer he was transferred to Ursula Beurton, codenamed 'SONYA', who was also handling Melita Norwood.

In 1943 Fuchs was sent to the United States to work on the Manhattan Project, reporting back to the GRU via spymaster Harry Gold in New York. While at the Los Alamos National Laboratory in New Mexico, where the atomic bomb was developed, Fuchs was able to pass on details of the atomic bomb and early models of the hydrogen bomb. The first Soviet atomic bomb was tested in Kazakhstan on 29 August 1949. Beria handed out lavish gifts to the scientists who had built it – though he also had a list of those who would go to the firing squad or the Gulag if they had failed. By the time Stalin died the Soviet Union had long-range bombers capable of dropping an atomic bomb on the United States. They were also on the threshold of making the hydrogen bomb that had been tested by the United States a year earlier, and the tense stand-off known as Mutually Assured Destruction had begun.

THE GULAG UPRISINGS

Following the death of Stalin, there was unrest in the Gulag. In May 1953, the inmates of the Gulag at Norilsk in Arctic Siberia withheld their labour. Although they had no weapons, and the protest was entirely peaceful, the MVD classified their action as 'an anti-Soviet and counter-revolutionary uprising'. The strike lasted 69 days. Technically the strike had been entirely legal. Nevertheless, the strikers were charged with 'mass insubordination… to the camp administration'.

That July, 18,000 of the 56,000 prisoners at the Vorkuta Gulag in the Komi Republic also went on strike. On 26 July, they stormed the punishment compound and released 77 prisoners, at which point the camp chief Derevyanko began the mass arrest of 'saboteurs'. The inmates responded with barricades, which prompted Derevyanko to order his men to open fire. Many died. The wounded were deprived of medical treatment and more died later. According to John Noble, an American arrested in Dresden after the Soviets seized his family's camera factory, the surrounding camps were also taken over by the inmates and 400 Red Army veterans tried to walk the 1,000 miles to Finland. They were intercepted on the way and killed.

In May and June 1954 there was an uprising at the Gulag at Kengir, central Kazakhstan, led by deported Ukrainians. After arming themselves they organized a propaganda campaign in which they claimed that they were pro-Soviet but opposed to the Beria-ites who ran the camps. Beria was now dead and disgraced, so the charge was a serious one. The inmates seized the food stores and then broke down the wall between the male and the female compounds. Jailed priests performed marriage services.

The inmates set up their own provisional government and ran their own affairs for 40 days. They had negotiations with MVD generals, in which they demanded a slight improvement in their conditions. While making concessions, the MVD sent in tanks, dogs and 1,700 troops in full battle gear. Survivors estimate that between 500 and 700 prisoners were killed, though the official figure was 37, excluding those who were executed or died of their wounds afterwards.

CHAPTER ELEVEN

STALIN'S CRIMINAL LEGACY

Although Stalin was dead, Stalinism was not. The murderous legacy of the Red Tsar would endure for a further 40 years or so in Russia. The Soviet Communist Party kept Stalin's brutal methods of control in place and they quickly crushed uprisings in satellite states. Russia would fight proxy wars around the world, while other dictators would continue to emulate Stalin by running oppressive dictatorships in the name of the people.

The Soviet Union with its empire of 800 million people stood still as Stalin's funeral took place and everybody feared for the future

ON 6 MARCH 1953, STALIN'S BODY LAY IN STATE IN THE HALL OF COLUMNS, A FEW STREETS FROM RED SQUARE. Over the following three days it is estimated that several million people trooped by to see him one last time. Several hundred people were said to have died in the crush.

Molotov, Beria and Khrushchev gave addresses at Stalin's funeral on 9 March 1953 and then the embalmed body was placed in Lenin's tomb in Red Square, alongside his old comrade. Lavrenty Beria now seemed to be in an unassailable position. His role as head of the newly-merged MGB and MVD meant that he not only commanded the secret police, a militia of 300,000 troops, the Gulag and its inmates and the Soviet spy network abroad, but he was also in charge of most of the Soviet Union's industry, including the secret nuclear bomb-making facilities. Others in the leadership were afraid of him – not least because he held potentially damaging dossiers on all of them.

Biding his time: Khrushchev with Stalin in 1936... if Stalin had known what was coming, Khrushchev would have been a dead man

NIKITA SERGEYEVICH KHRUSHCHEV (1894–1971)

The son of a coal miner, Khrushchev was born in the Russian village of Kalinovka in 1894 and brought up in Ukraine where he went to work as a pipe fitter at the age of 15. As a factory worker, he was exempt from conscription in the First World War. Before 1917, he was active in various workers' organizations and in 1918 he joined the Bolsheviks. In January 1919, he joined the Red Army as a political commissar.

A full-time Party worker in Ukraine, he came to the attention of Stalin's associate Lazar Kaganovich, who invited him to the Fourteenth Party Congress in Moscow. In 1929 he moved to Moscow to study metallurgy at the Stalin Industrial Academy, where he became secretary of the academy's Party Committee. He supervised the completion of the Moscow underground, winning the Order of Lenin.

A fervent supporter of Stalin, he was one of three provincial Party secretaries to survive the Great Purge and he went on to join the Politburo. In 1940, he supervised the integration of eastern Poland into the Soviet Union, at the same time liquidating the Polish and Ukrainian nationalist movements. When Germany attacked the Soviet Union in 1941, he supervised the evacuation of Ukraine's industry. He served as political adviser to Marshal Yeremenko during the Battles of Stalingrad and Kursk.

After the Soviet Union had re-established control in Ukraine, he became first secretary of the Ukrainian Communist Party. His efforts to restore Soviet control and increase agricultural production earned him the nickname 'Butcher of the Ukraine'. When Stalin died in 1953, Khrushchev engineered the arrest and execution of Beria. He then removed Malenkov and brought the security services under the control of the Council of Ministers, before travelling abroad to seek *rapprochement* with Tito.

On the night of 24 February 1956, Khrushchev made a 'secret speech' to a closed session of the Twentieth Congress of the Communist Party of the Soviet Union condemning Stalin's 'abuse of power'. Khrushchev's words led to the release of millions of political prisoners and greater freedom of speech, albeit briefly. There were also revolts in Poland and Hungary. Although these were put down forcibly, Khrushchev continued his reform agenda at home and abandoned the traditional demand for world revolution. He also preached peaceful co-existence with the West – during his visit to the United States in 1959, he flew to Hollywood to have lunch with Marilyn Monroe. 'Khrushchev looked at me like a man looks at a woman,' she said later.

Despite his call for peaceful co-existence, Khrushchev oversaw the Cuban missiles crisis, in which the Soviet Union installed nuclear missiles on Cuba and then withdrew them. He also created a very public split with Communist China, though he negotiated a nuclear test-ban treaty with the United States. However, his softening stance led to a palace coup, following which he was deposed by his protégé and deputy Leonid Brezhnev in October 1964.

The Fall of Beria

Just a month after Stalin's death, Beria released those who had been arrested in connection with the 'Doctors' Plot'. The official statement was that 'the basis of the charges against them of anti-Soviet and espionage activity is lacking'. Two of the doctors had died under torture and the others were physical and mental wrecks. Their torturer, Mikhail Dmitrievich Ryumin, was arrested and executed. Also known as 'the Midget', he was the man who first 'uncovered' the plot. Working together, Beria, Malenkov and Khrushchev put an end to Stalin's anti-Semitic witch-hunt. A statement in *Pravda* accused former MGB agents of causing 'national dissension and undermining the unity of the Soviet people which had been welded together by internationalism'. But the seeds of anti-Semitism sown by Stalin did not just disappear. The MVD took back none of the Jewish officers it had purged in the early 1950s and it banned the recruitment of any fresh Jewish agents.

Beria then made a series of mistakes. First of all, he appointed the trusted but inexperienced Lieutenant-General Vasili Stepanovich Ryasoy as head of the Foreign Directorate. Ryasoy then recalled all of the Party's foreign representatives to Moscow to discuss future policy, which served to identify them to Western intelligence services.

On 17 June 1953, violence erupted in the German Democratic Republic (GDR). On the previous day, construction workers in East Berlin had gone on strike in response to the government's threat to cut their pay if they did not meet higher quotas. Their numbers quickly swelled and a general strike was called. Some 40,000 protesters gathered in East Berlin calling for free elections and the reversal of Stalinist policies. The East German government called for Soviet support, troops were sent in and many protesters were killed.

Normally, the MVD kept such things in check so Beria flew to Berlin to find out what had gone wrong. While he was away, a meeting of the Presidium was called. Beria hastened back to find himself accused of mismanaging the situation. He had permitted the first serious challenge to Communist Party rule in the Soviet bloc and had jeopardized Russian dominance in eastern Europe.

Khrushchev began plotting Beria's downfall. He had managed to get Premier Malenkov and Defence Minister Bulganin on to his side, but more importantly the Red Army supported him. They had suffered appallingly from Beria's repeated purges of their ranks. Then Molotov and Beria's deputy, Sergei Kruglov, were talked round. The others were given the story that Beria was going to be demoted to minister for petroleum.

On 26 June 1953 Beria was called to a special meeting of the Presidium. His wife Nina warned him to be careful, but he was confident that Molotov was still on his side. Fearing the worst, Khrushchev attended the meeting with a gun in his pocket.

SERGEI NIKIFOROVICH KRUGLOV (1907–77)

Born to a peasant family, Kruglov joined the Communist Party in 1928. In 1938, he joined the NKVD, where he investigated and prosecuted other members of the NKVD as part of the Great Purge. During the early months of the Great Patriotic War, he organized Blocking Detachments, which stood behind the front line troops to prevent them from retreating. He then oversaw the mass execution of men accused of desertion or unauthorized retreat. As first deputy of the People's Commissar of Internal Affairs, he was in charge of the Gulag and he also organized the mass deportation of Chechens and Ingushes from the north Caucasus. This earned him the Order of Suvorov, first class, a medal usually only awarded for exceptional bravery at the front.

In 1944, Kruglov prepared the NKVD report on the Katyn massacre, blaming it on the Germans. Then he was sent to Lithuania, where he put down the partisans who opposed the country's annexation by the Soviet Union. In 1945 he was promoted to the rank of colonel general. After successfully organizing the security at the Yalta conference, he was awarded the United States Legion of Merit and the British KBE, thereby becoming the only Soviet intelligence officer to be given an honorary knighthood.

After replacing Beria as head of the MVD in 1946 he allied himself with Viktor Abakumov, who had been appointed head of the MGB in the same year. The two appointments were thought to have been a deliberate ploy by Stalin to undermine Beria. In 1948, Kruglov organized the mass deportation of the German population of the Kaliningrad Oblast, formerly East Prussia. Stalin then approved the Kruglov–Abakumov plan to toughen conditions in the Gulag and prevent the imminent release of those who had been sentenced to ten years during the Great Purge. He was awarded the Order of Lenin for supplying Gulag labour to the nuclear programme.

Following Beria's arrest in 1953, Kruglov became minister for internal affairs, but he only lasted until 1956, when he was ousted by a Khrushchev loyalist. After serving in a series of progressively more lowly posts, he was stripped of his general's pension and turned out of his government accommodation. His death in 1977 is shrouded in mystery. Some sources maintain that he died after being accidentally hit by a train, while others say that he committed suicide or died of a heart attack.

At the meeting, Bulganin and Khrushchev began attacking Beria.

'What's going on, Nikita?' asked Beria. 'Why are you searching for fleas in my trousers?'

He then turned to Malenkov.

'What's on the agenda today?' he asked. 'Why have we met so unexpectedly?'

At this point Malenkov's nerve failed him so Khrushchev took over.

'There is only one item on the agenda,' he said, 'the anti-Party, divisive activity of imperialist agent Beria.'

The motion was put that Beria should be removed from the Presidium, dropped from the Central Committee, expelled from the Party and arrested. Molotov and Bulganin voted in favour of the proposal. When it was time for Malenkov to speak, he pushed a secret button under the desk and Marshal Zhukov burst in with a bunch of army officers who seized Beria. A division of tanks and riflemen surrounded the Kremlin to prevent the MVD from rescuing him.

Guarded by 50 armed men, Beria was bundled into a black government car. He was then forced to lie on the floor while he was driven at top speed to a secret prison on Osipenko Street, where he was kept in a small windowless cell with the lights burning day and night. The NKVD were not told what had happened to him so his henchmen were easily rounded up. It was only on 10 July that Beria's arrest was announced in *Pravda*. Claiming all of the credit, Malenkov stated that Beria was being held for 'criminal activities against the Party and the State'. In December, it was said that Beria and his six accomplices were in the pay of foreign intelligence agencies and had for years been 'conspiring to seize power in the Soviet Union and restore capitalism'.

Meanwhile Beria wrote to his former colleagues. He begged for his life and

The anti-bandit squad of the Volksovskaya Cheka *from the Kharkov region in 1920: they were the forerunners of all the forces of repression that would terrorize the Soviet Union for many decades to come*

THE ORIGINS OF THE KGB

Established in 1954, the KGB – *Komitet Gosudarstvennoy Bezopasnosti* or Committee for State Security – was the last and most enduring of the Soviet security agencies. These began in 1917 with the Cheka – originally the VCHEKA, *Vserossiyskaya Chrezvychaynaya Komissiya po Bor'bye s Kontr-revolyutsiyei i Sabotazhem* or 'All-Russian Extraordinary Commission for Struggle Against Counter-revolution and Sabotage'. This organization quickly assumed responsibility for imprisoning or executing the nobility, the bourgeoisie, the clergy and anyone who was considered an 'enemy of the state'. A merciless tool of the Communist Party, its job was to put down anti-Soviet rebellions. With a manpower of over 250,000, the agency was responsible for killing more than 140,000 people.

In 1922, the Cheka was replaced by the GPU – the *Gosudarstvennoye Politicheskoye Upravlenie* or State Political Administration – in an attempt to end the Cheka's reign of terror. Then in November 1923 the GPU became the OGPU – *Ob'edinennoe Gosudarstvennoe Politicheskoe Upravlenie* or Unified State Political Administration – which kept the population under surveillance and ran 'corrective' labour camps.

By the 1930s, the organization had recruited informers in government departments, factories and the Red Army. It also conducted covert operations abroad, kidnapping and murdering the regime's opponents.

As Stalin consolidated power, the OGPU became the NKVD – the People's Commissariat of Internal Affairs – which conducted the Great Purges, executing more that 750,000 people in 1937–38 alone, including tens of thousands of Party officials, as well as the NKVD's first two chiefs, Genrikh Yagoda and Nikolay Yezhov. Lavrenty Beria took over in 1938.

In 1941, responsibility for state security passed from the NKVD to the NKGB – the People's Commissariat for State Security. The agencies then became ministries, with MVD head Beria also overseeing the MGB. Under Beria's deputy Viktor Abakumov, the MGB ensured the loyalty of the Red Army's officer corps, ran the prisoner of war camps and deported the ethnic minorities. At the same time, it was responsible for foreign intelligence in Nazi Germany, through the 'Red Orchestra' spy ring, and among the Western Allies – the Cambridge Five and other agents worked for the MGB.

After the war, the MGB crushed all opposition in the occupied countries of eastern Europe, as well as the Soviet Union. Between 1945 and 1953, over 750,000 Soviet citizens were arrested and punished for 'political crimes' and it is estimated that by 1953 around 2,750,000 Soviet citizens had been jailed or sent to the Gulag, with a similar number in internal exile.

The MVD and the MGB were reunited after the death of Stalin, but the role of the MVD dwindled when the prisoners were released from the Gulag and it was abolished in 1960. Meanwhile, all security duties were taken over by the newly formed KGB.

asked them to find the lowliest job for him. 'You will see that, in two or three years, I'll have straightened out fine and will still be of use to you,' he wrote. 'I ask the comrades to forgive me for writing in a somewhat disjointed fashion and badly because of my condition, and because of the poor lighting and not having my pince-nez.'

Beria and his cabal were tried by a special session of the Supreme Court. They were given no defence counsel and no right of appeal. According to the indictment they had aimed to 'revive capitalism and restore the rule of the bourgeoisie'. It was alleged that Beria had been working for British intelligence until the moment of his arrest, though no evidence was presented to support this claim.

The former security chief was found guilty of offences that stretched back to 1919, when he had worked in the security service of the short-lived Azerbaijan Democratic Republic (ADR), a Muslim parliamentary democracy that had been recognized by the United States and Britain. However, Lenin was anxious to secure the vital Baku oilfields so in 1920 the ADR was invaded by the Red Army.

Beria was also convicted of terrorism because of the execution of 25 political prisoners without trial in 1941, part of the purge of the Red Army ordered by Stalin. Then there were several counts of treason. First, he was convicted of an attempt to open peace talks with Hitler in 1941, via the Bulgarian ambassador. There was no mention of the fact that he was acting on the orders of Molotov and Stalin. Then he was convicted of trying to hand the northern Caucasus over to the Germans, even though he had organized its defence in 1942. Furthermore, in order to seize power he now planned to hand parts of the Soviet Union over to other countries – the Kaliningrad Oblast to Germany, parts of the Karelian Isthmus to Finland, the Moldavian Soviet Socialist Republic to Romania and the Kuril Islands to Japan. His habit of raping women and girls was alluded to as 'crimes which testify to his moral degradation'.

Found guilty on all counts, he and the other defendants were shot on 23 December 1953. According to some accounts he fell to his knees and begged for mercy, while other sources relate that he faced death with some dignity. He was dressed in a black suit when he died – though his mouth was stuffed with bandages, or perhaps a towel, to prevent him from making a last statement. His body was then burnt and his ashes scattered. His wife Nina was sent to the Gulag in Sverdlovsk. Released in 1954, she died in exile in Siberia in 1991. In the great Stalinist tradition Beria became a non-person. His image was airbrushed from photographs and subscribers to the *Great Soviet Encyclopaedia* were told to remove his entry and replace it with a reference to the Bering Sea.

One of the criticisms of Beria was that he intended to liberalize the Soviet Union, while those around him had been brought up with Stalinism. With his death, the iron grip of the dead tyrant took hold once more. In March 1954, the KGB was formed to take over the state security apparatus. From its headquarters in Moscow's Dzerzhinsky Square its tentacles spread through the government and then across the Soviet bloc from the border with West Germany to the Bering Straits. Its training centre for spies in Leningrad then enabled it to spread far beyond its home territory.

What Soviet citizens wrote, read or thought was controlled by the Chief Administration for Safeguarding State Secrets in Print, or *Glavlit*. This organization censored newspapers, journals and books.

Movement was also closely regulated. At the age of 16, Soviet citizens were required to obtain an internal passport, which allowed them to travel from one part of the country to another. Although some political prisoners were released from the Gulag after the death of Stalin, they were soon replaced. The KGB could arrest anyone for being 'politically unreliable' and a month's unemployment also earned a term of imprisonment.

The Post-Stalin Thaw

Although Stalinism appeared to be continuing unabated, things were nevertheless changing. On the night of 24 February 1956 Khrushchev made a 'secret speech' to a closed session of the Twentieth Congress of the Communist Party of the Soviet Union, in which he condemned Stalin and his methods. During the speech Khrushchev recalled Lenin's long-suppressed Testament, which foretold Stalin's abuse of power. Then he cited numerous examples to prove Lenin's point. During the Great Purge, Khrushchev said, many entirely innocent Communists had been tortured into making confessions before being imprisoned or executed.

The purge of the Red Army had weakened an essential resource, while Stalin had made inadequate preparations for war and had mishandled its conduct. Khrushchev went on to condemn the mass deportations, Stalin's policy on Yugoslavia, Stalin's intention to purge the Jews and the cult of personality he had created to glorify his leadership.

However, Khrushchev did not condemn collectivization, the mass terror or any other abuses of power that he himself had been implicated in. Instead, he sought to smear his political rivals through their association with Stalin's excesses. Nevertheless it was clear that the Soviet Union recognized some, if not all, of Stalin's crimes.

The speech was never published, but it was read at local closed meetings of the Party. It caused shock and disillusionment throughout the Soviet Union and the Eastern Bloc. People were not just outraged by Stalin himself, but by the entire Stalinist system he had left behind. In Poland, there was a general strike and the offices of the secret police were attacked. After the strike had been put down by force, Khrushchev and other Soviet leaders visited Warsaw and threatened invasion. Nevertheless, Polish Communist leader Wladyslaw Gomulka – who had been denounced by Stalin for 'national deviation' and imprisoned – was returned to power and concessions were granted. The experience of Poland emboldened the Hungarians and the Hungarian Uprising followed.

Under Khrushchev, artistic censorship was also lifted. Boris Pasternak feared for his life during the Great Purge and his works were banned, yet after Stalin's death he went on to publish *Doctor Zhivago*. His novel won the Nobel Prize in 1958, though the award aroused so much opposition in the Soviet Union that he refused it. Khrushchev later admitted that Pasternak's death had been hastened by the Soviet response to his Nobel Prize success.

Khrushchev then encouraged the publication of Aleksandr Solzhenitsyn's *One Day in the Life of Ivan Denisovich*, which portrayed life in the Gulag. After Khrushchev fell from power in 1964, Solzhenitsyn's works could not be published in the Soviet Union. However, manuscript copies circulated inside the country and his books were published in the West. In 1970, he was awarded the Nobel Prize for Literature, but he refused to go to Stockholm to collect it, believing that the Soviet authorities would prevent him from re-entering the country.

When the first volume of *The Gulag Archipelago* – an attempt to document the whole of the labour-camp system – was published in Paris in 1973, Solzhensitsyn was pilloried in the Soviet press. Arrested and charged with treason on 12 February 1974, he was deported a day later. There was now no reason not to claim his Nobel Prize, so he picked it up in Stockholm the following December. After moving around Europe he eventually settled in Vermont, USA. With the advent of *glasnost* (openness), his work was published in the Soviet Union once more. His Soviet citizenship was restored in 1990 and he returned to Russia in 1994.

Hungarian Uprising

After the death of Stalin, the hardline Hungarian premier Mátyás Rákosi had been replaced by Imre Nagy, who promised the release of all political prisoners and an end to collectivization and the forced development of heavy industry. Instead, he promised more consumer goods. However, in the spring of 1955, Nagy was forced from office and expelled from the Party. Rákosi was then reinstated, but he was dismissed again in July 1956 when Nagy was returned to office. This time Nagy promised the abolition of the one-party state and the withdrawal of Soviet troops. On 23 October, the day of Nagy's appointment as the head of a coalition which included the Independent Smallholders' Party, the Social Democrats and the National Peasant Party – who even had a 'Catholic association' – some 200,000 students took to the streets demanding the reforms that the Poles had been granted.

The protesters took over the radio station and then broadcast 16 demands – one of them being the dismantling of the giant bronze statue of Stalin in the city park of Budapest. A hundred thousand protesters descended on the statue whose inscription described Stalin as Hungary's 'best friend'. A protester placed a sign over

Stalin's mouth that read, 'RUSSIANS, WHEN YOU RUN AWAY DON'T LEAVE ME BEHIND!' Then the crowd chanted 'Russia, go home!' and pulled the statue down.

According to Budapest's police chief, Sándor Kopácsi,

'They placed a thick steel rope around the neck of the 25-metre tall Stalin's statue while other people, arriving in trucks with oxygen cylinders and metal cutting blowpipes, were setting to work on the statue's bronze shoes... An hour later the statue fell down from its pedestal.'

Graffiti was then daubed on the remains of the statue. KGB chief Ivan Serov arrived in Budapest that day and demanded to know why the 'fascist and imperialist' protesters had not been shot down. Police Chief Kopácsi pointed out that the protesters were the young intelligentsia, the hope for the future, who merely considered they were fighting for human rights.

'I'll have you hanged from the highest tree in Budapest,' Serov said.

On 25 October 1956, Soviet tanks fired on the protesters. Dozens were killed and around 150 were wounded. This turned the demonstrators into a revolutionary mob and peasants reoccupied their confiscated fields. The army supported the demonstrators, even handing out arms from their depots. Communist leaders were hanged from trees, political prisoners were released and Cardinal Mindszenty was escorted back to his palace by a cheering crowd.

Nagy demanded that the Soviet troops leave Hungarian soil and he was told that they were being withdrawn. Then on 1 November he announced that Hungary was leaving the Warsaw Pact – Communist eastern Europe's mutual defence alliance, which had been set up

IVAN ALEKSANDROVICH SEROV (1905–90)

The first chief of the KGB, Serov joined the Red Army in 1923. Surviving the Great Purge, he was the executioner of Marshal Tukhachevsky and other Red Army leaders. It is also thought that he was in charge of the execution of Nikolay Yezhov.

After joining the NKVD in 1939, Serov helped organize the mass deportations from the Caucasus, the Baltic States and Poland. It is thought that he was also responsible for the Katyn massacre. As Beria's deputy he conducted mass arrests in Poland after the Warsaw Uprising of 1944 and he co-ordinated the mass expulsion of the Crimean Tartars.

As a deputy to Viktor Abakumov, Serov played a leading role in SMERSH, from which position he introduced Stalinism to Poland, establishing the secret police there and organizing the persecution of the Polish Home Army.

In 1954, Serov became head of the KGB, when he was instrumental in putting down the Hungarian Uprising. Four years later he was moved to the GRU but he was dismissed after the 1962 Cuban missile crisis and in 1965 he was stripped of his Party membership.

Crowds jeer on the streets of Budapest in 1956 as a member of the secret police is strung up by the mob during the insurrection

the year before to counter NATO. He asked the United Nations to recognize Hungary's neutrality under the joint protection of the great powers. However, despite assurances to the contrary the Red Army did not withdraw. Instead, five fresh divisions were on their way to Hungary.

On the night of 3 November Hungary's defence minister, Major-General Pál Maléter, and his staff were invited to the Soviet military headquarters, ostensibly to discuss troop withdrawals. A lavish banquet had been laid on. At midnight Serov burst in. Flanked by KGB officers, he was brandishing a pistol. The Red Army seized the airfields and the junctions on the main highways and on the following day Soviet tanks entered Budapest. Protesters were shot down and the wounded were tied to the fronts of the tanks as a warning to others. Nagy and several of his ministers sought asylum in the Yugoslav Embassy and others, including Police Chief Kopácsi, were arrested as counter-revolutionaries.

Janos Kádár, Nagy's deputy, formed a government on 21 November. He abandoned the reform agenda and declared Hungary a 'dictatorship of the proletariat' – Stalin's stated aim. Kádár assured those that had taken refuge in the Yugoslav Embassy that they could go home unmolested. However, when they

THE COLD WAR

The Cold War was the stand-off between the Soviet Union and the West following the Second World War. In 1945 the uneasy alliance between Stalin and the Western Allies began to unravel. First of all, there was conflict over the return of prisoners of war and displaced persons. And then Britain and America began to believe that Stalin would not live up to his promise to allow free elections in eastern Europe. The 1945 ceasefire line that ran across Europe from the Baltic to the Adriatic solidified into an armed frontier between the Communist East and the democratic West. Churchill dubbed it the 'iron curtain'.

The term 'Cold War' was first used in a US congressional debate in 1947. Then the United States increased its influence in western Europe with aid provided under the Marshall Plan, while the Soviets installed Communist governments in the countries to the east. Relations between the two sides became openly hostile during the blockade of Berlin in 1948–9. In response, the United States and her European allies formed the North Atlantic Treaty Organization (NATO), a mutual defence pact.

In 1949 the Soviet Union exploded its first atomic bomb, ending the United States' monopoly. That same year the Communists took control of China and in 1950 Soviet-backed North Korea invaded South Korea, beginning the Korean War.

Cold War tensions eased slightly with the death of Stalin and the ceasefire in Korea. However, in 1955 the Soviet Union and the Communist countries of eastern Europe countered NATO with the Warsaw Pact. That year the Communists took over Cuba and anti-colonial movements around the world embraced Communism.

In 1958, the threat of conflict intensified with the development of intercontinental ballistic missiles and nuclear stockpiles. The separation of East and West Germany became complete with the building of the Berlin Wall in 1961. A year later, the Soviets began secretly installing missiles on Cuba, which gave them the ability to launch nuclear attacks on American cities. The Cuban missile crisis, a confrontation between the US and the Soviet Union, brought the world to the brink of war until Khrushchev agreed to withdraw the missiles. There followed a nuclear test-ban treaty in 1963.

Another theatre of war developed in 1965, when the United States sent troops to confront the Soviet-backed Hanoi government in Vietnam. This led to the humiliating United States withdrawal in 1973 and the takeover of the whole of Vietnam, Laos and Cambodia by the Communists in 1975. However, the confrontation between the United States and the Soviet Union eased with two strategic arms limitation treaties.

When Mikhail Gorbachev came to power in 1985, he began dismantling the old Stalinist system. The Soviet Union relaxed its grip on the countries of eastern Europe and the Communist regimes fell. This was followed by the collapse of Communism in the Soviet Union and its breakup into 15 separate nations. The Cold War was at an end.

emerged they were seized by Soviet officers and handed over to the KGB. One minister died under torture and another went on hunger strike and starved himself to death. Nagy and Maléter were tried in secret and executed.

East is East and West is West

Stalin's intransigence had prevented the unification of Germany as envisaged by the Potsdam Agreement, so in 1949 West Germany became the Federal Republic of Germany (FRG), while East Germany paradoxically became the German Democratic Republic (GDR). With help from the Marshall Plan, the FRG thrived but with its factories denuded by the Soviet Union the economy of the GDR faltered. East Germans flocked into the West, looking for a better life. However, the border between the GDR and the West was part of the 'iron curtain' and it was heavily armed. Stalin had justified the closing of the border between the Soviet zone of occupation and the Western zones as a defence against the forces of imperialism, but the fleeing East Germans could still cross through Berlin.

In the years between 1949 and 1961 some two and a half million Germans moved from the East into the West. The loss of skilled workers and professional

Divided city: the Berlin Wall was constructed in 1961, separating West Berlin from East Berlin and the rest of Germany. It was really put up to stop East Berliners from defecting to the West, but the Communists called it 'The Anti-Fascist Protection Wall'

people threatened to destroy the economic viability of East Germany so on the night of 12 August 1961 work started on a wall that would divide East and West Berlin. In the East, it was known as the 'Anti-Fascist Protection Wall', thereby implying that the people in East Germany needed protection from their West German neighbours.

Although the Soviet bloc was now completely cut off from the West, there were still some anti-Stalinist forces at work. In 1961, the biggest monument to Stalin – a massive granite statue 15.5 metres high and 22 metres long, which had been erected in Prague – was destroyed. The sculptor Otakar Švec, who had been working under immense pressure from the government and the secret police, had received hate mail from a number of Czech citizens, which had driven him to commit suicide three weeks before the statue was unveiled. The monument became an embarrassment to the Communist Party of Czechoslovakia who blew it up – this was no easy task; it required 800kg of explosives [*see illustration on page 178*].

The Thaw Ends

The thaw ended when Khrushchev was forced from power in 1964. Stalinism reasserted itself under Leonid Brezhnev and the Soviet Union's satellite states once more came under pressure.

In January 1968, reformer Alexander Dubcek came to power in Czechoslovakia. First of all he undertook to democratize the Communist Party and make all offices open to election and then he promised 'socialism with a human face'. The freedom of the press was re-established while apolitical youth clubs and the Boy Scout movement were revived.

On 27 June, an article appeared in *Literární listy* (Literary Gazette) urging rapid progress to real democracy. It was signed by people who had been drawn from all walks of life. A special meeting of the Warsaw Pact, which Dubcek refused to attend, warned that Czechoslovakia was on the verge of counter-revolution. Brezhnev then summoned Dubcek to a meeting in a small town in Slovakia.

A communiqué issued after the meeting gave the impression that the pressure on Czechoslovakia would be eased if the press was reined in. However, on 20 August 1968 Warsaw Pact forces entered Czechoslovakia and Dubcek and the other leaders were taken to Moscow. Dubcek was unseated in April 1969 and in 1970 he was finally expelled from the Party. He was replaced by the 'realist' Gustáv Husák who began the process of 'normalization'. Meanwhile Brezhnev propounded the 'Brezhnev Doctrine' which asserted the right of the Soviet Union to intervene when the 'essential common interests of other socialist countries are threatened by one of their number'. In 1979, he used this as an excuse to invade Afghanistan and prop up the failing Communist government there.

Dubcek returned to prominence in 1989 after the Communist Party gave up its monopoly on power. He died under suspicious circumstances on 7 November 1992.

Memorial wall to those killed in the Stalinist purges, Moscow, 1988: in 2003, a poll revealed that 53 per cent of Russians continued to believe that Stalin had mainly played a 'positive' role in Russian history

On 1 January 1993 Czechoslovakia was split into the Czech Republic and Slovakia.

Stalin's Ghost Lives On

Brezhnev died in 1982, after a long physical and mental decline. He was replaced by 70-year-old Yury Vladimirovich Andropov, the first KGB chief to become Party leader. He lasted 15 months and was replaced by 72-year-old Konstantin Ustinovich Chernenko, who died after a year in office. Then came Mikhail Sergeyvich Gorbachev, the first Soviet leader to have been born after the October Revolution. The son of a peasant family, Gorbachev believed that socialism could be achieved without Stalinist repression. He began the policies of *perestroika* (restructuring) and *glasnost* (openness). However, by drawing the veil aside, Gorbachev had once more allowed the people of the Soviet bloc to see how badly they had been mistreated. Calls for national independence came from the countries of eastern Europe and the trend spread to Ukraine, Georgia, Armenia and Azerbaijan, which had been under Soviet domination since the Russian Civil War. And there was talk of the re-unification of Germany within NATO.

Meanwhile, Gorbachev was dismantling the totalitarian state that Stalin had spent his lifetime building. Then on 9 November 1989 protesters broke through the Berlin Wall and began to tear it down.

But there were still Stalinists about, who predicted the break-up of the Soviet empire. And *perestroika* threatened the lucrative careers that had been built up in the Stalinist era. Vladimir Kryuchkov, head of the KGB, feared that the security service would be slimmed down and broken up, with its powers being spread around the individual republics. On

Dmitry Ustinov with Yuri Andropov, the first former KGB chief to become Party leader – he was 70 years old and only lasted 15 months

17 June 1991 he made a speech in parliament, saying that Gorbachev's cordial dealings with the West were proof that he intended to destroy the Soviet Union. There was a mole, he said, inside the Kremlin.

In August, Gorbachev and his wife were taking a holiday in their dacha in the Crimea when Kryuchkov formed an eight-man State Emergency Committee and attempted a coup. The Gorbachevs were held under house arrest for three days. However the Chairman of the Supreme Soviet for the Russian Soviet Republic, Boris Yeltsin, took a stand against the plotters. After organizing widespread opposition to the coup he jumped on to a tank and harangued the soldiers who came to occupy the city.

The forces of reaction? Tanks occupied Red Square as the Gorbachevs were confined in their dacha in the Crimea for three days, but Boris Yeltsin saved the day for the new freedoms when he successfully intervened, repelling the invasion

The coup collapsed and Gorbachev and his wife were freed. But the leader of the Soviet Union had lost any authority. On 24 December 1991 the Russian Federation took the Soviet Union's seat at the United Nations. Gorbachev resigned a day later and the Union of Soviet Socialist Republics was officially dissolved.

As president of Russia, Boris Yeltsin was the first popularly elected leader in the country's history. But still the ghost of Stalin hung over Moscow. When Yeltsin resigned in 1999 his prime minister, Vladimir Vladimirovich Putin, a former member of the KGB, took over as acting president. Promising to rebuild a weakened Russia, Putin was elected

Vladimir Putin is another in the long line of Soviet strong men – pulling the strings behind Medvedev

president in his own right in 2000. After two terms in office he stood down and his chosen successor Dmitry Anatolyevich Medvedev took over. Putin then became prime minister – many think he is the power behind the throne.

Putin was popular in Russia for his strong-man image. And Stalin had not been entirely repudiated, for Putin unveiled a bust commemorating the former dictator and then went on television praising his wartime role. According to a survey in 2009, more than 35 per cent of Russians believed that Stalin's leadership during the Great Patriotic War vindicated the 'mistakes' he made during his murderous reign. Almost as many people believed that Russia still needed a leader like him. Meanwhile, the Russian Communist Party formed the second biggest party in parliament.

In 2009, supporters celebrated the 130th anniversary of Stalin's birth by laying wreaths at his grave by the Kremlin wall while Party leaders compared his 'immortal' achievements to those of Peter the Great and Lenin. A handbook for history teachers emphasized his role as 'an effective manager' and state-controlled TV documentaries marking the 70th anniversary of the start of the Second World War paid generous tribute to 'Uncle Joe'. Only last year a state-sponsored contest to identify Russia's greatest historical figure put Stalin in third place.

'He was our saviour,' said Viktor Ilyukhin, a Communist MP. 'If it was not for him we would have had a German Buchenwald in the Urals and Siberia.'

Putin's own assessment of Stalin was ambiguous. He urged people to weigh up the dictator's good and bad points.

'In my view, you cannot make one overall assessment,' he said. 'Any historical events need to be analyzed in their entirety.'

May Day, 2010: the cult of Stalin persists in Moscow. Russian president Dimitry Medvedev, however, insisted that the mass exterminations of the Stalin era could not be justified on any basis

Timeline

21 December, 1879: Later to be known as Stalin, Josef Vissarionovich Dzhugashvili is born in the city of Gori, Georgia

1894: Stalin enrolls in Tiflis Theological Seminary and rebels against being forced to speak Russian

1899: After being expelled, Stalin takes on board the writings of Lenin and becomes a Marxist revolutionary

1902: Stalin is arrested for the first time and sent to Siberia

1903: The Social-Democratic Party splits into two groups – Stalin joins the Bolsheviks rather than the Mensheviks

1905: Stalin meets Lenin for the first time at the Bolshevik conference in Finland

1906: Stalin marries Yekaterina Svanidze

1907: Birth of Stalin's first child, Yakov; his wife Yekaterina dies of typhoid

1912: Stalin is appointed by Lenin to the Central Committee of the Bolsheviks after their official separation from the Social Democrats

1913: Stalin writes *Marxism and the National Question* for Lenin

1914: Outbreak of WWI

1917: The tsar's government falls, Lenin returns from Switzerland and the Bolsheviks overthrow the Provisional Government. Stalin backs Lenin in the Russian Revolution

1918: Stalin marries Nadezhda Alliluyeva

1918-20: Civil War in Russia – Stalin is in charge of armed forces in St Petersburg

1921: Stalin's second son, Vasily, is born; Stalin plays a major role in the invasion of Georgia by the Red Army

1922: The USSR is born; Stalin becomes General Secretary of the Communist Party; Lenin suffers his first stroke

1923: Lenin warns the Party against Stalin, then suffers a second stroke

1924: Lenin dies; Stalin survives the reading of Lenin's testament, denounces Trotsky and launches his theory of 'Socialism in One Country', eschewing internationalism

1926: Stalin attacks the United Opposition of Zinoviev, Kamenev and Trotsky at the 15th Party Congress; birth of Stalin's daughter, Svetlana

1927: First Five-Year Plan; Zinoviev, Kamenev and Trotsky are expelled from the Party (Trotsky is exiled to Central Asia), leaving Stalin in absolute control of the Soviet Union

1929: Stalin attacks Bukharin who is later removed from the Politburo; Stalin announces that class enemy the *kulaks* must be eliminated as collectivization begins

1931-32: Famine across the USSR

1932: Stalin's second wife, Nadezhda Alliluyeva, dies, but is it suicide or murder?

1934-38: The Great Terror

1935: Zinoviev and Kamenev are arrested after being framed for Kirov's assassination by Leonid Nikolaev – many believe that Stalin ordered Kirov's murder

1936: First show trial – Zinoviev, Kamenev and their allies confess and are executed

1937: Second show trial; purge of the Red Army

1939: At 18th Party Congress, Stalin announces the end of the Great Terror; the Nazi-Soviet pact is signed in Moscow; WWII begins

1940: Trotsky is assassinated in Mexico City

1941: Hitler invades USSR; soon after, Stalin addresses the Soviet Union, with the wild claim that the Germans have lost 4.5 million troops to the USSR's 350,000. He maintains that victory is within the Soviet Union's grasp.

1942-43: Defeat in the Battle of Stalingrad marks the beginning of the end for Hitler; Stalin meets Churchill and US President Franklin D. Roosevelt in Tehran to discuss military strategy

1944: Churchill and Stalin meet in Moscow to discuss the future of Europe

1945: Stalin meets Roosevelt and Churchill in Yalta; Hitler commits suicide in the Berlin bunker, ending war in Europe; the USSR controls the whole of eastern Europe; the USA drops two atomic bombs on Japan, precipitating the end of war in the Pacific region

1948: Communists gain control

of Czechoslovakia

1949: The USSR tests its first nuclear bomb; Stalin is 70; Mao Zedong and the Communists win the Chinese Civil War

1950: Sino-Soviet Treaty; Korean War begins, with Stalin providing military help to North Korea

1953: Announcement of Jewish Doctors' Plot against Stalin as part of a new wave of terror; after an all-night dinner with Beria, Malenkov, Bulganin and Khrushchev, Stalin collapses. He has had a stroke which paralyzes the right side of his body. He dies on 5 March.

1956: Khrushchev attacks Stalin's cult of personality

1967: Stalin's daughter, Svetlana Alliluyeva, defects to the USA

INDEX